THE PENCIL DRAWINGS OF

THE PENCIL DRAWINGS OF

Joe Belt (signature)

TEXAS TECH UNIVERSITY PRESS
LUBBOCK

Library of Congress Cataloging-in-Publication Data

Belt, Joe, 1949-
    The pencil drawings of Joe Belt.
      p.   cm.
    ISBN 0-89672-180-9   ISBN 0-89672-181-7 (pbk.)
    1. Belt, Joe, 1949-   2. Southwest, New, in art. I. Title.
NC139.B434A4 1988
741.973—dc 19   88-25996
                                             CIP

Printed in the United States of America

Texas Tech University Press
Lubbock, Texas 79409-1037 USA

I don't remember where I first met Joe Belt—maybe at Mesquite's Cafe or at the Lubbock Arts Festival—but I had been aware of his work for years. Joe had the reputation of being a "good and fast" commercial artist. He has always been very versatile, possessing strong design and illustration skills.

Good illustrators have always fascinated me: N. C. Wyeth, Remington, Russell, Von Schmidt, Harvey Dunn, Dean Cornwell—are they "fine artists" or "illustrators"? I don't know. I like their work. They make me want to go paint. When I was teaching at Texas Tech, I'd take my students to The Museum, and, regardless of the exhibit, I'd wander over to the section that had the Nicholai Fechins and Peter Hurds, artists with whom I felt I had a kinship.

I feel a kinship with Joe Belt's work, all of which relies on drawing, strong design, and value pattern. I love good value orchestration, where the lights and darks of the picture lead the eye first to the focal point, the "star" of the picture, and then around to the "supporting actors" of the piece. Joe, as a "matter-of-fact" artist of the American Southwest, does this very effectively. His straight-forward, undramatic approach to western subjects is reminiscent of Gordon Snidow and Robert "Shoofly" Shufelt. At this juncture, Joe is a master of the necessary skills: drawing, design, and painting techniques. Ahead of him is his further unfoldment as an artist. The more personal Belt becomes in his work, the more universal will be his appeal.

Paul Milosevich
May 1988

To my wife, Kathy, and children, Brandi, Jennifer, and Cody, for their never-ending love and support.

I don't remember not
wanting to draw. I think it is
the challenge of bringing a
surface to life with a pencil
and a sheet of paper. With
very few tools, the artist has
to add depth, dimension,
texture, shading, lights,
darks, expression, character,
feeling, and that spark of
life.

Joe Belt
June 1988

LIST OF DRAWINGS

MISSIN' TWO, 1987
From a roundup on the old Matador Ranch
14½" x 21"
Joe Belt
Lubbock, Texas

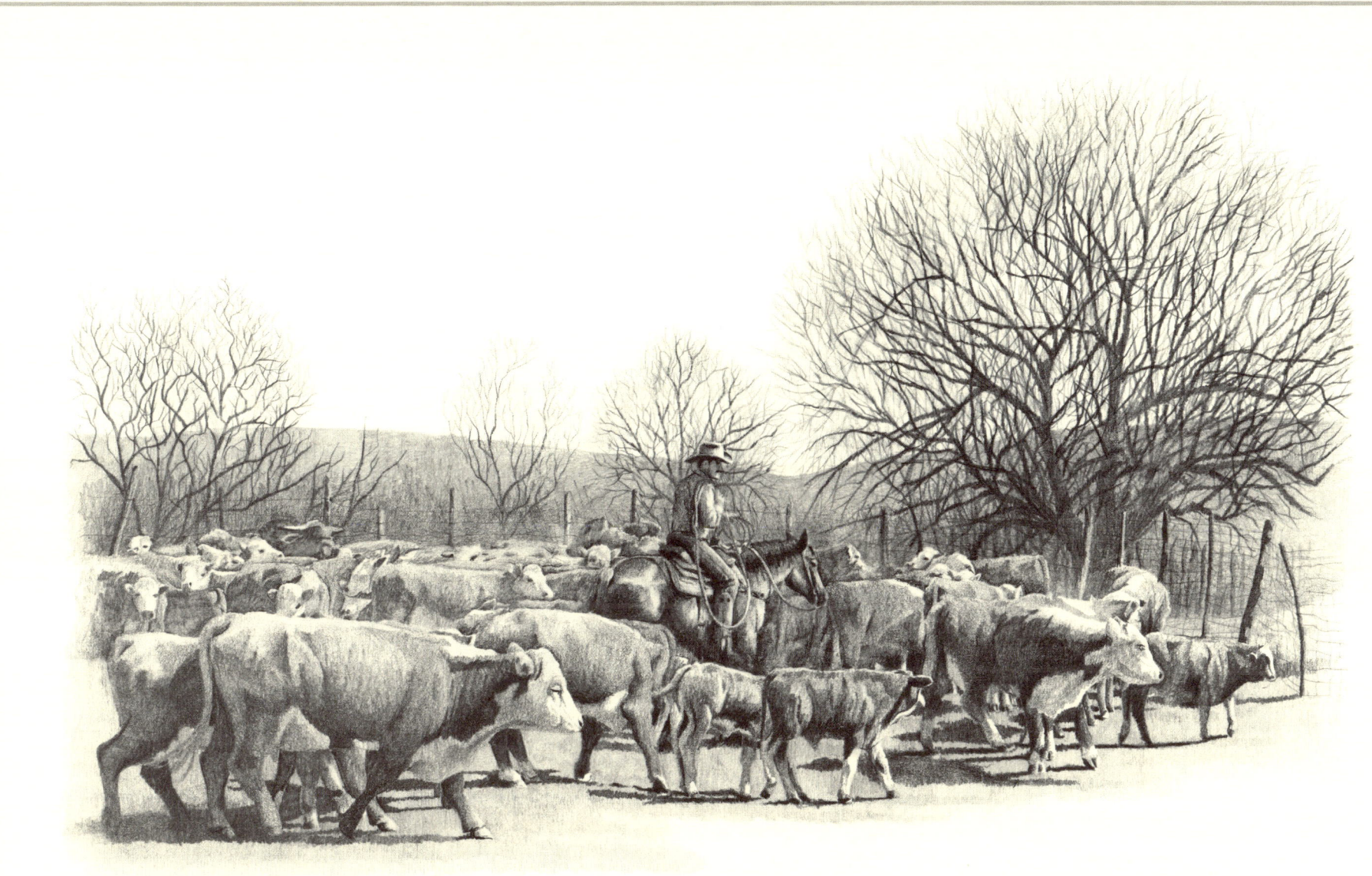

"MISSIN' TWO"

Joe Belt
NWA

2

SIOUX CHIEF, 1985
9½" x 11"
John and Nadine Madden
Denver City, Texas

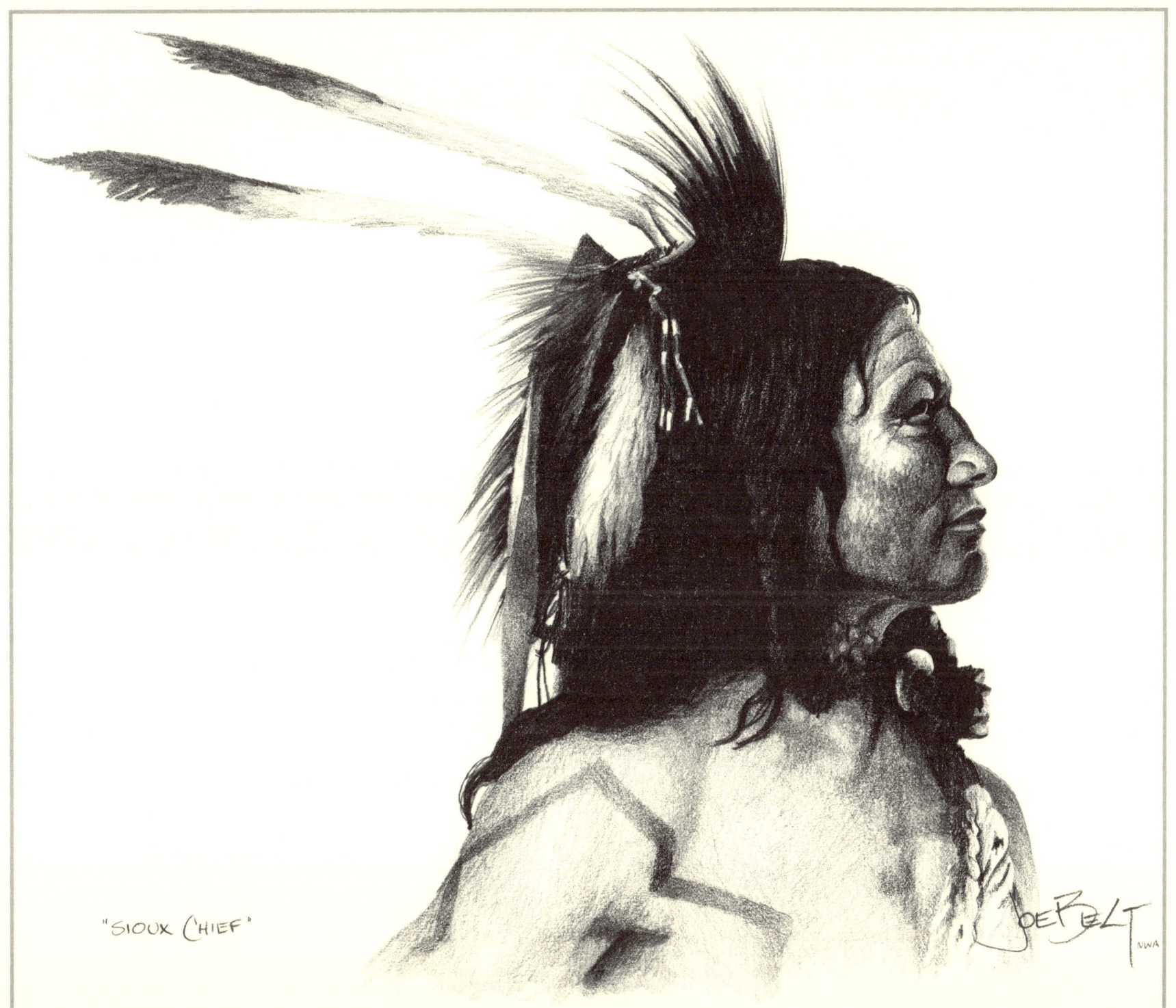

"SIOUX CHIEF"

UNTITLED, 1985
5" x 7"
Mr. and Mrs. Charles J. Propst
Post, Texas

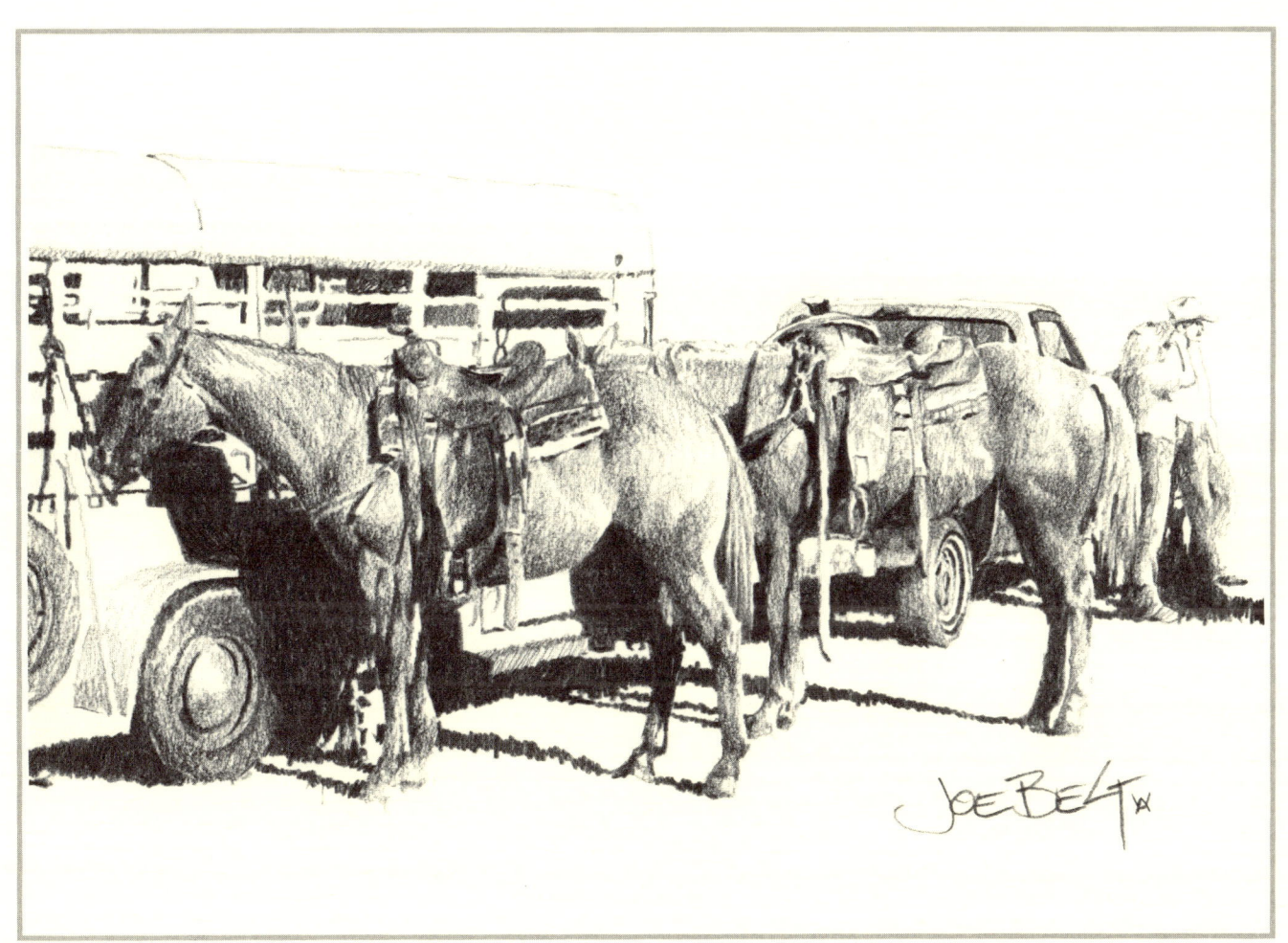

4

RAMSKULL, 1988
7" x 9"
Mr. and Mrs. John Truby
Woodrow, Texas

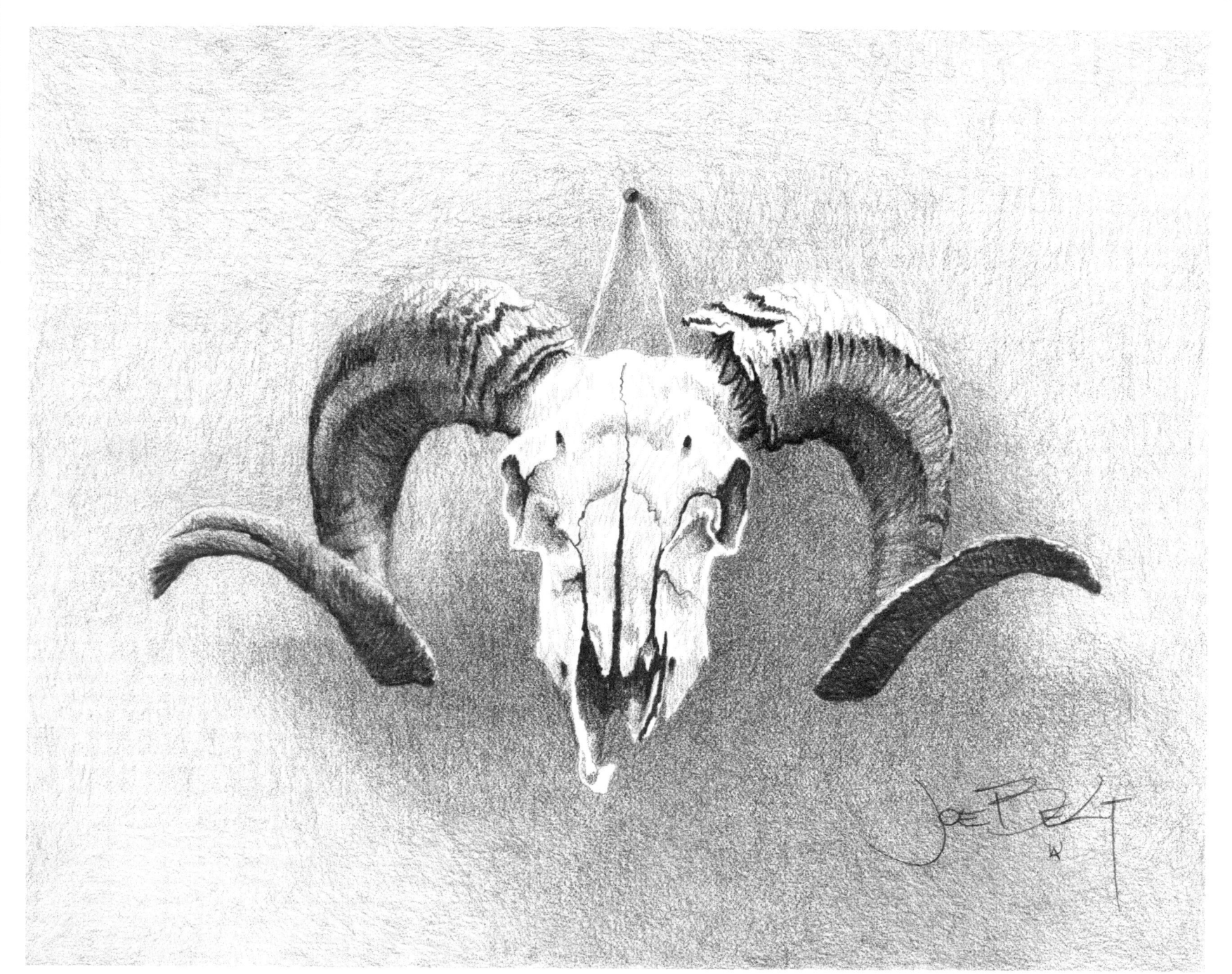

5

INDIAN GIRL, 1987
2½" x 5"
Mr. and Mrs. John Truby
Woodrow, Texas

6

WHITE ANTELOPE, 1988
Indian Lady in Edmond, Oklahoma
7" x 9"
Gregory Cassell
Granada Hills, California

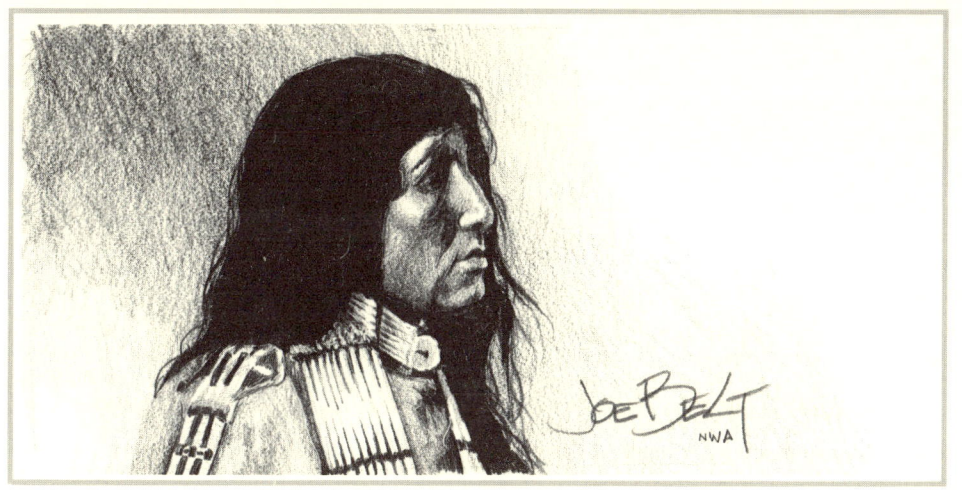

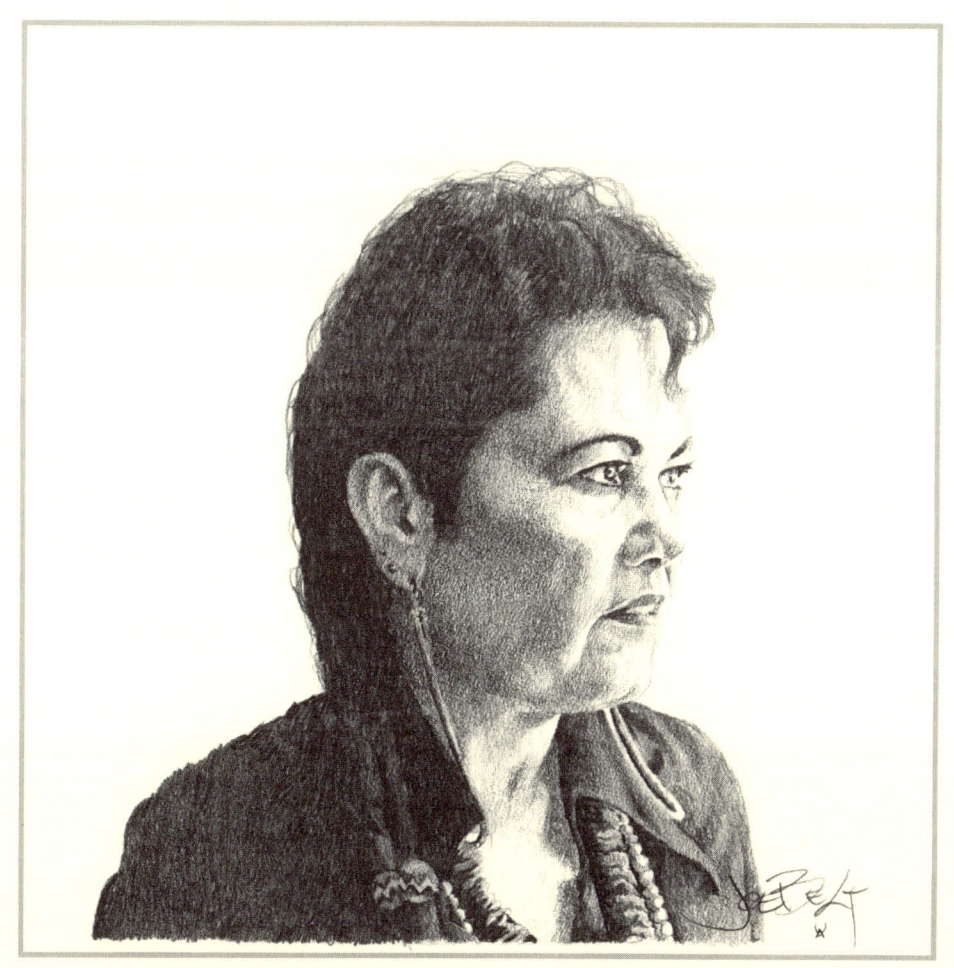

7
TOOTER, 1988
A friend from high school
10″ x 10″
Joe Belt
Lubbock, Texas

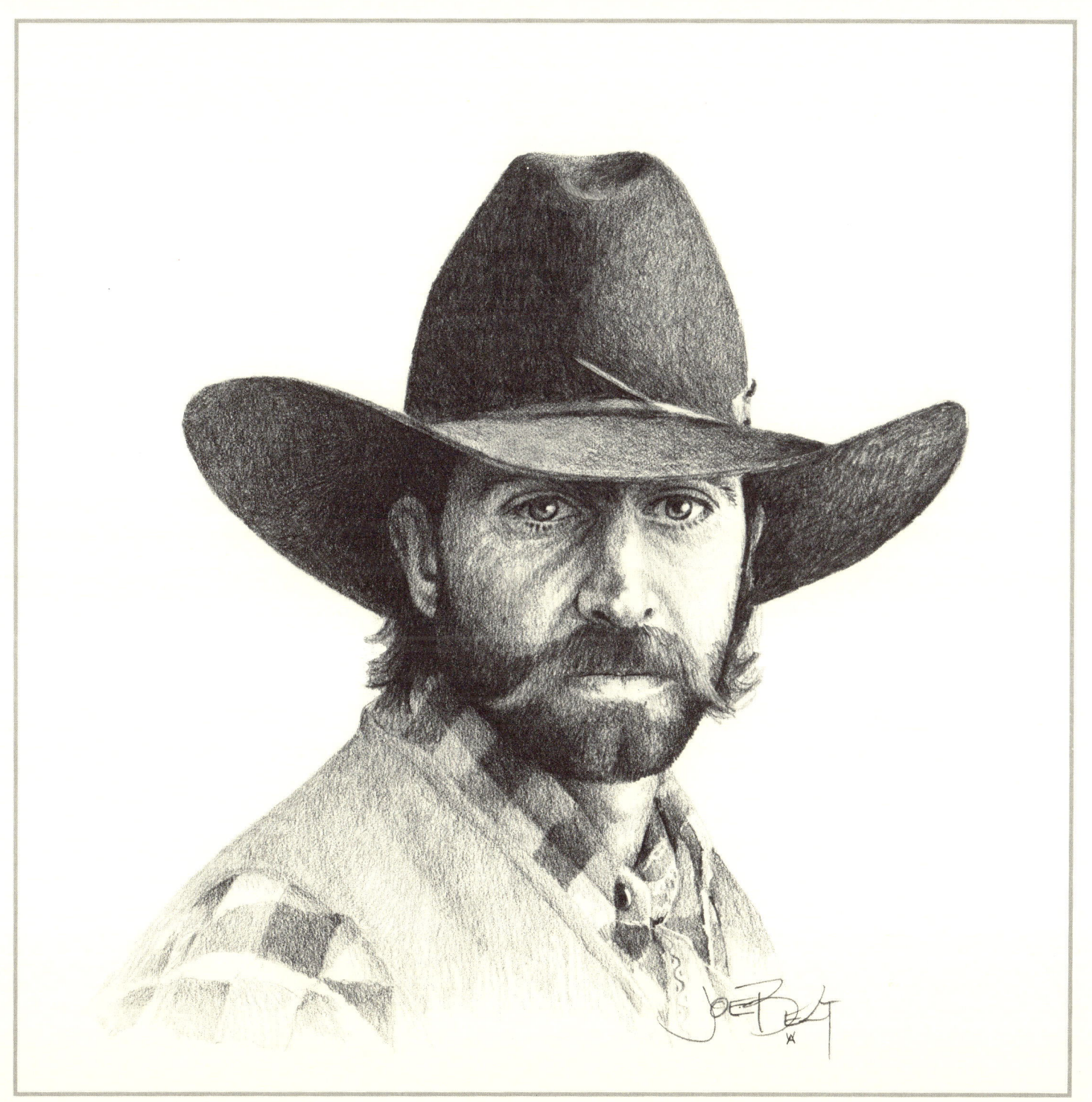

8

SOMEDAY, 1983
18" x 24"
Mr. and Mrs. Bill Price
Lubbock, Texas

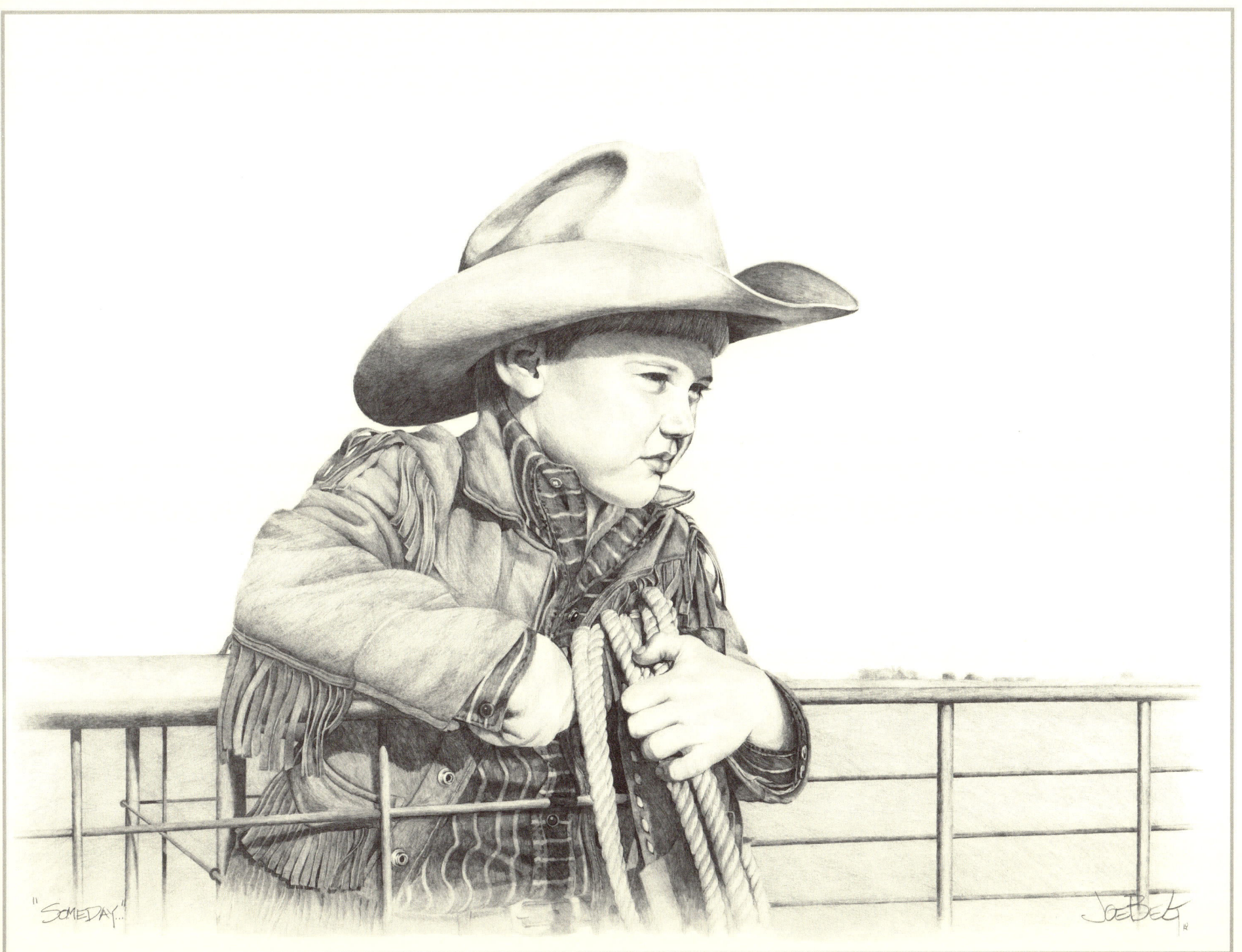

"Someday..."

Joe Belt

9

UNTITLED, 1987
An adobe in Taos, New Mexico
7¼" x 9½"
Marilyn Lee
Oklahoma City, Oklahoma

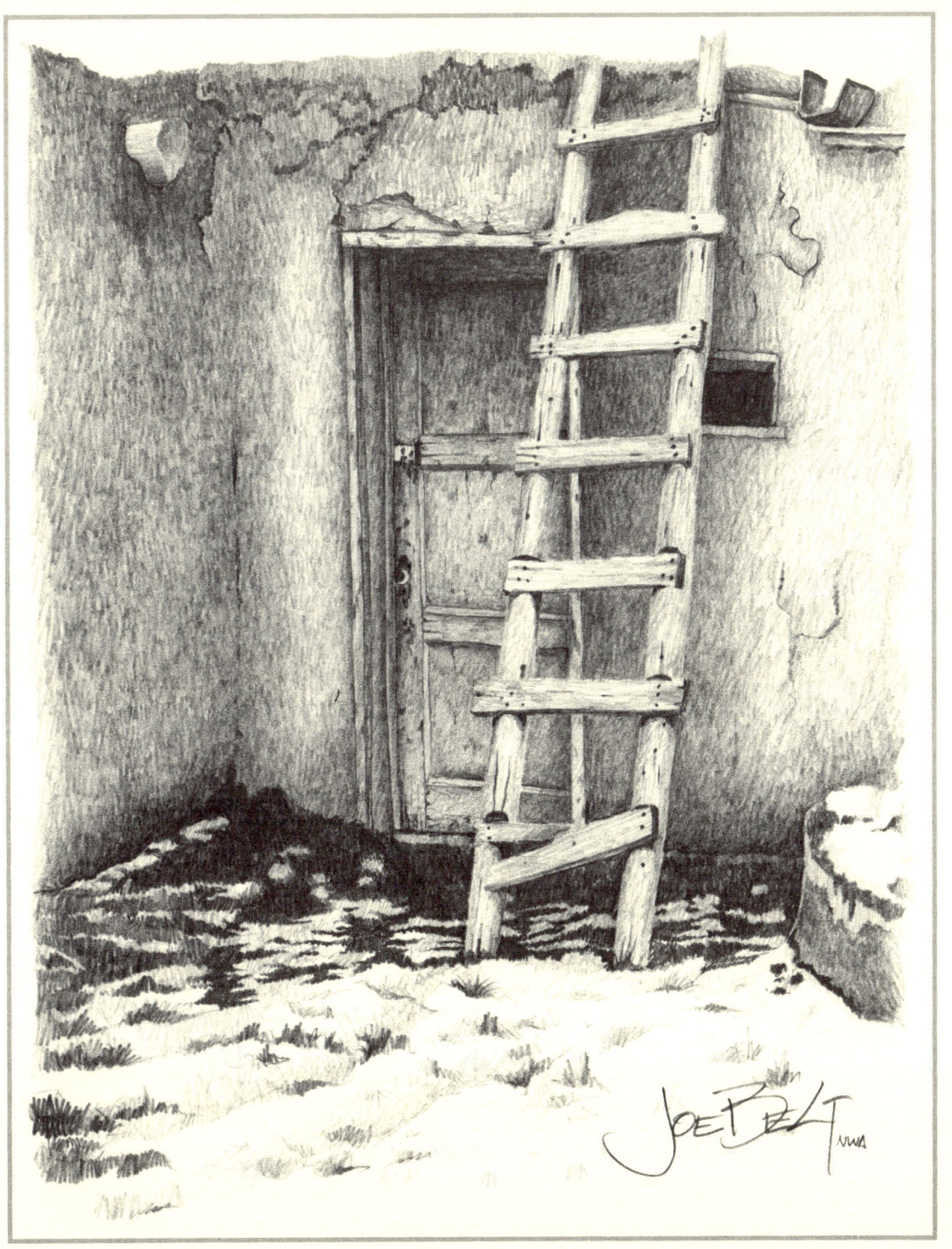

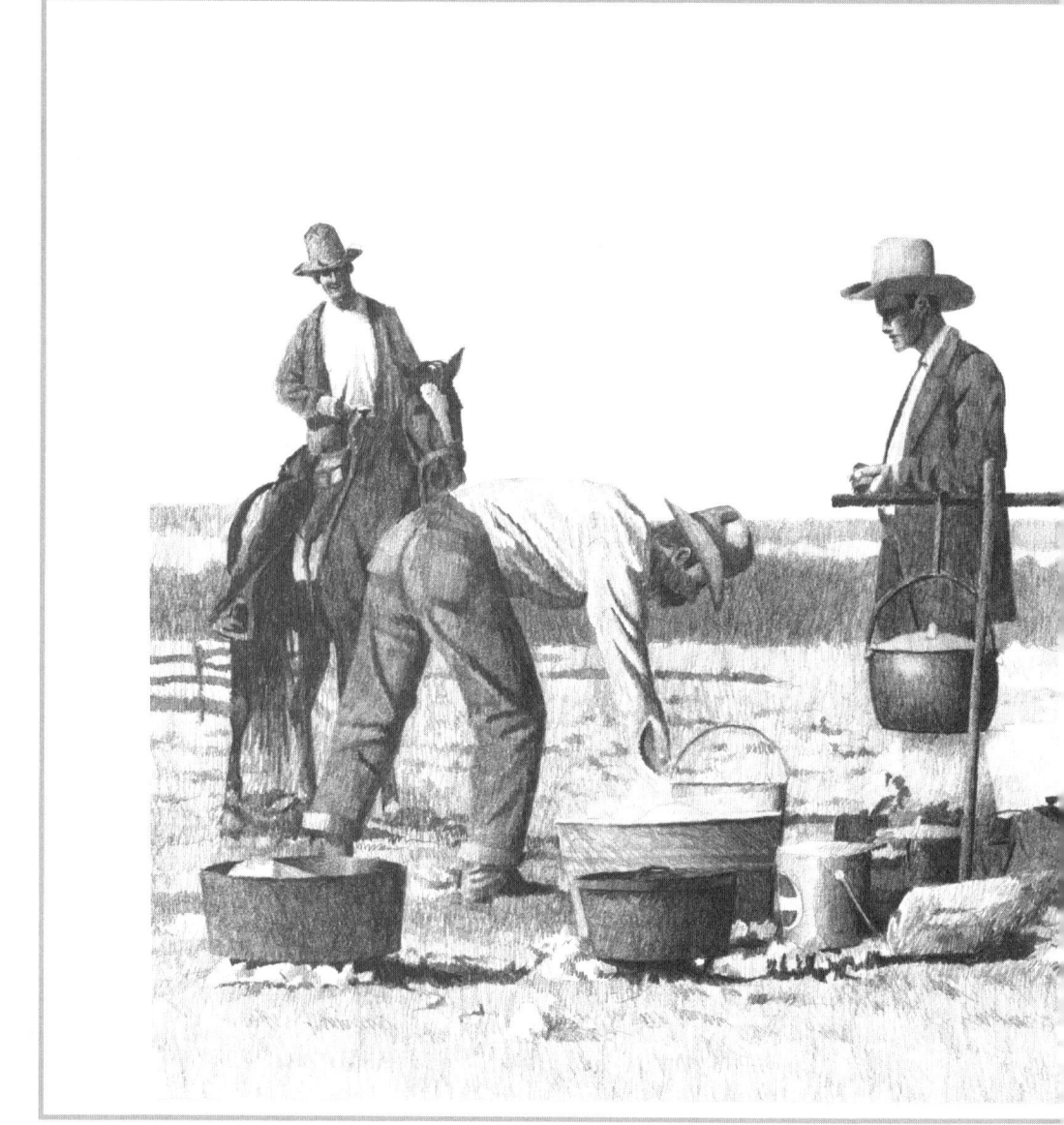

10
'BOUT SUPPERTIME, 1985
From a historical photo
10" x 26½"
Mr. and Mrs. David Tuohy
San Diego, California

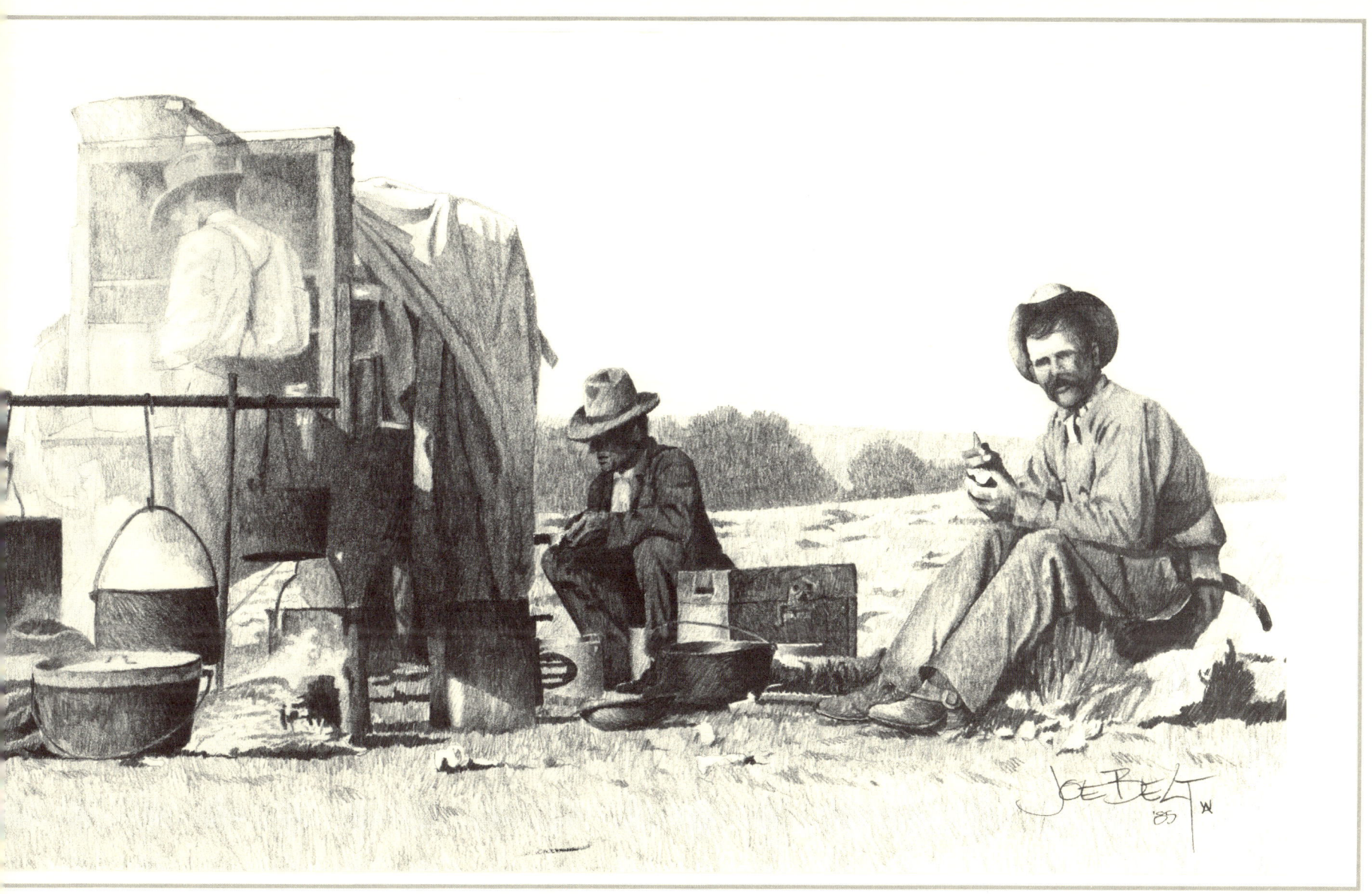

PUEBLO STRAY, 1987
A dog wanting in, Taos, New Mexico
8" x 11"
Cynthia Cope
Oklahoma City, Oklahoma

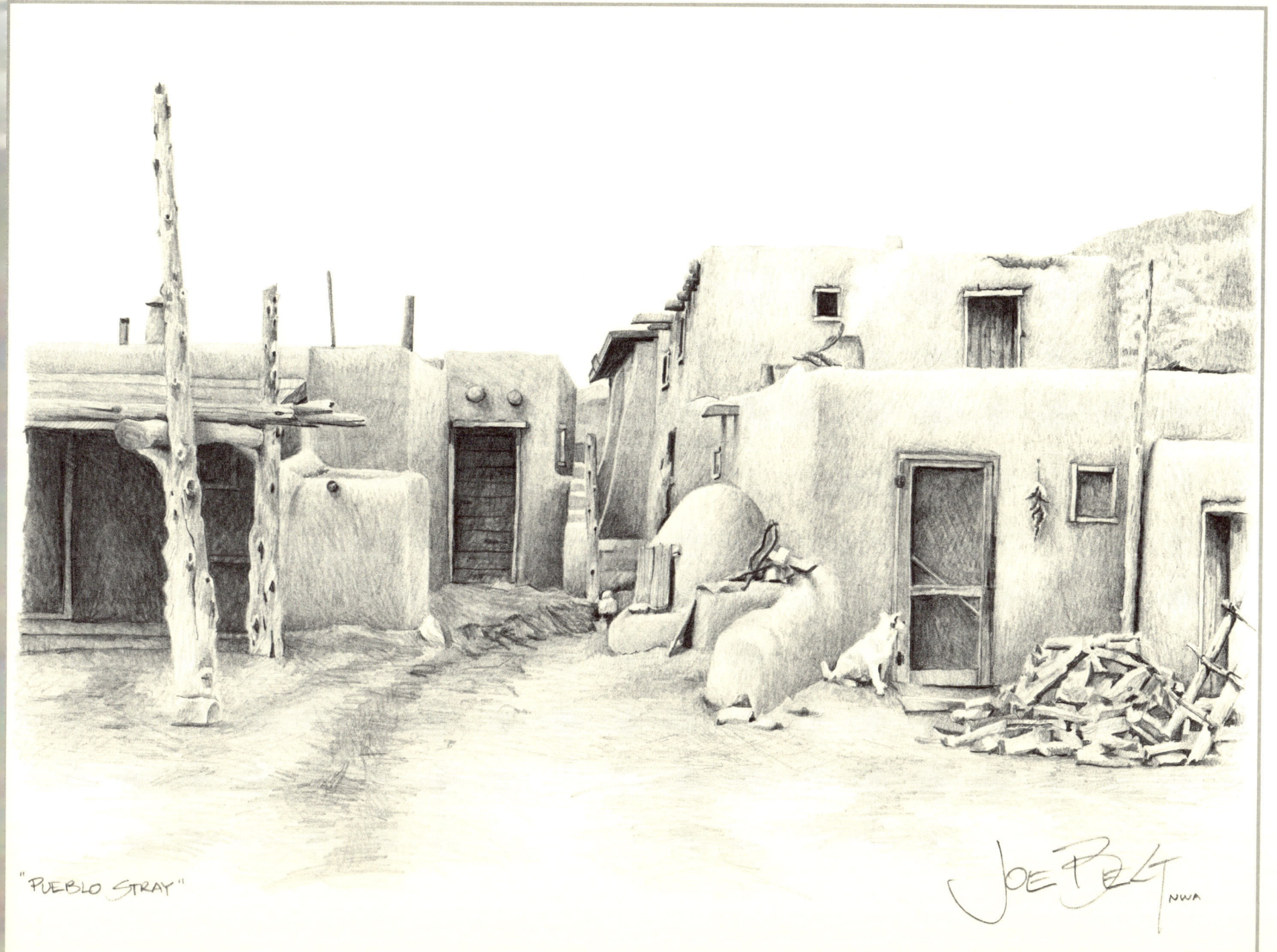

"PUEBLO STRAY"

JOE BELT NWA

12

UNTITLED, 1988
A spring roundup and branding at the Pitchfork Ranch
8" x 10"
Mr. and Mrs. Bob Moorhouse
Guthrie, Texas

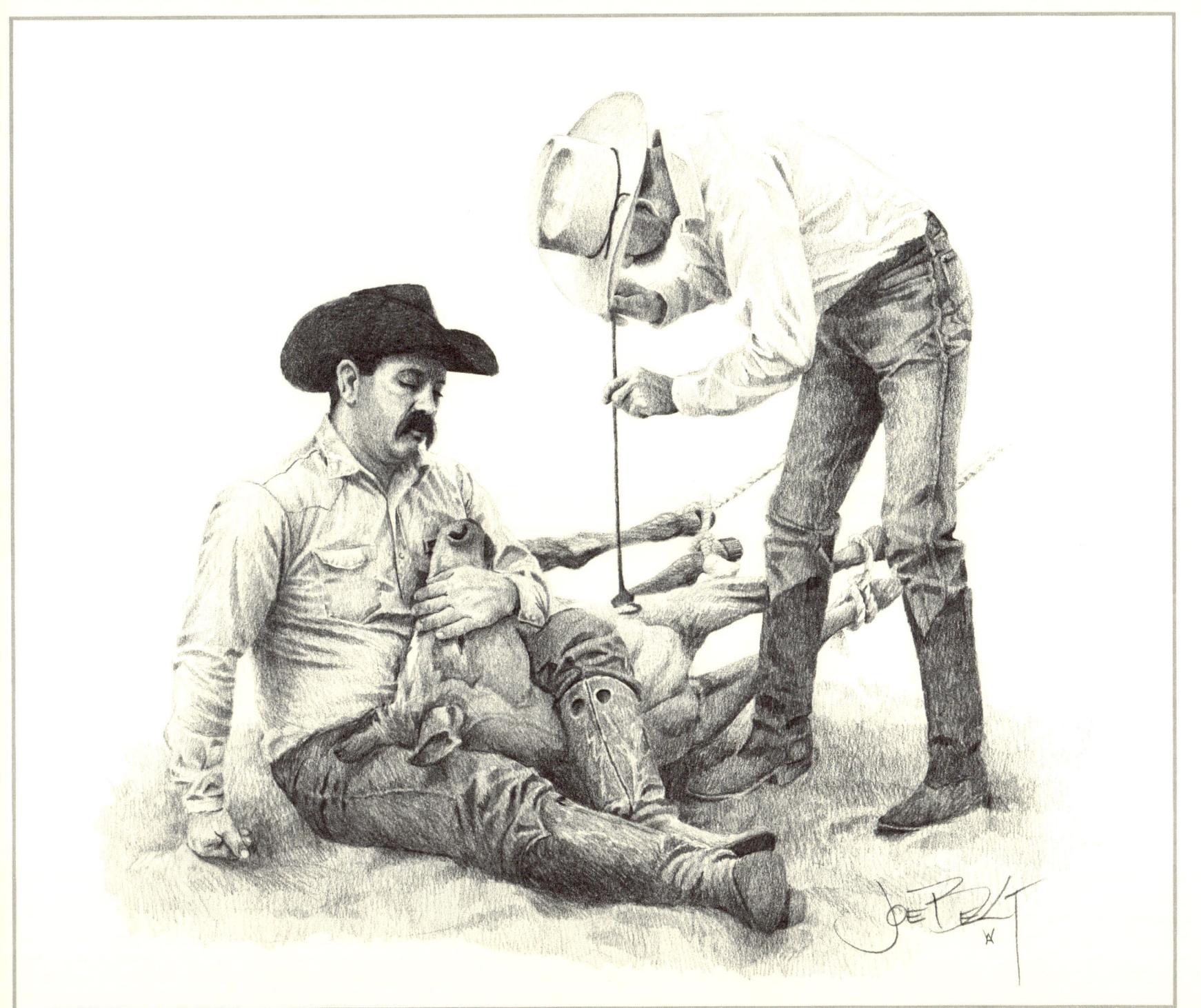

13
FRED AND HIS COWDOG, 1985
Part-time cowboy/school teacher from Fluvanna, Texas
13" x 17"
Mr. and Mrs. Claude R. Cage
Colorado Springs, Colorado

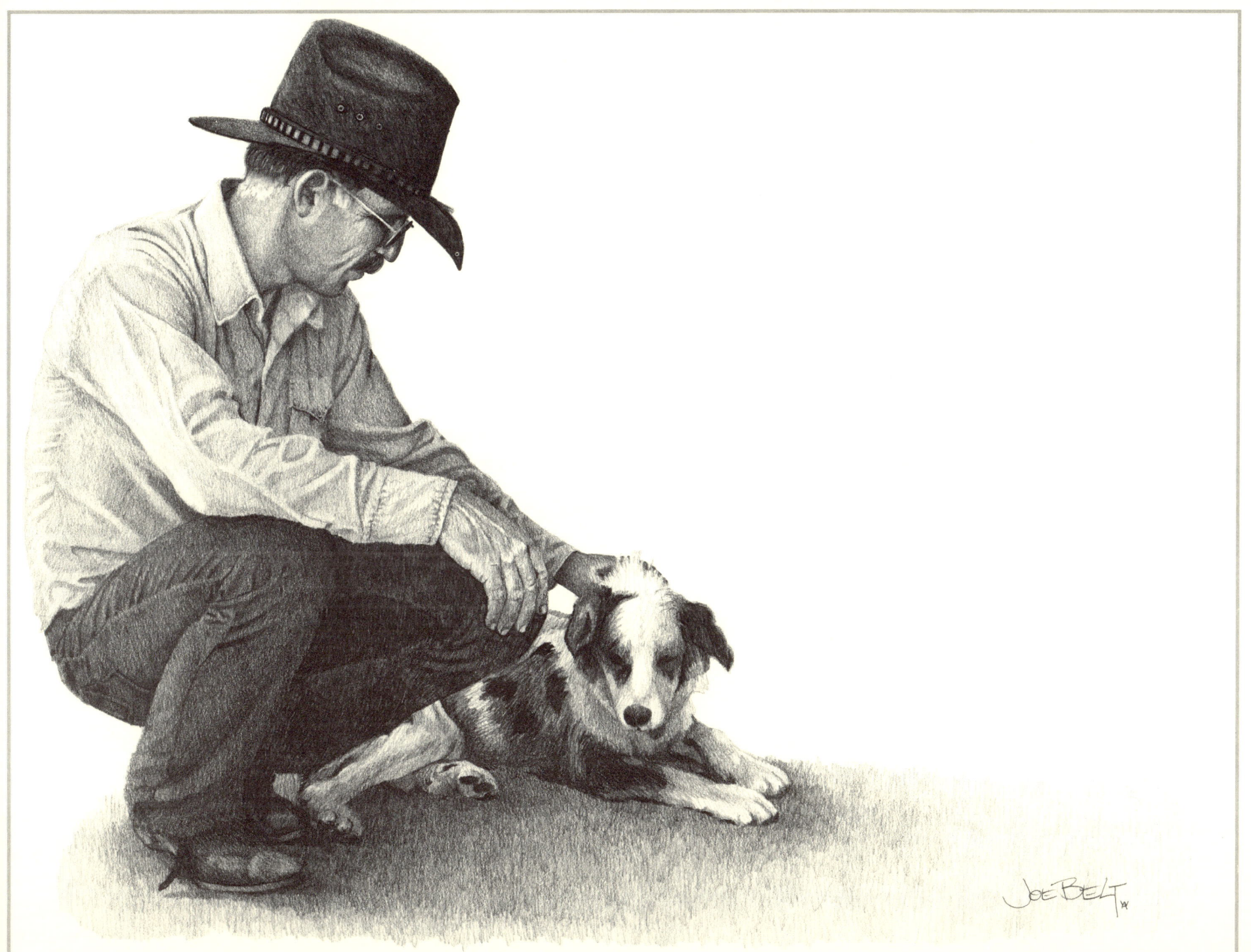

Joe Belt

14

RESTIN', 1986
Cowboy from around Dickens, Texas
5" x 7"
Mr. and Mrs. Jimmy Avery
Crosbyton, Texas

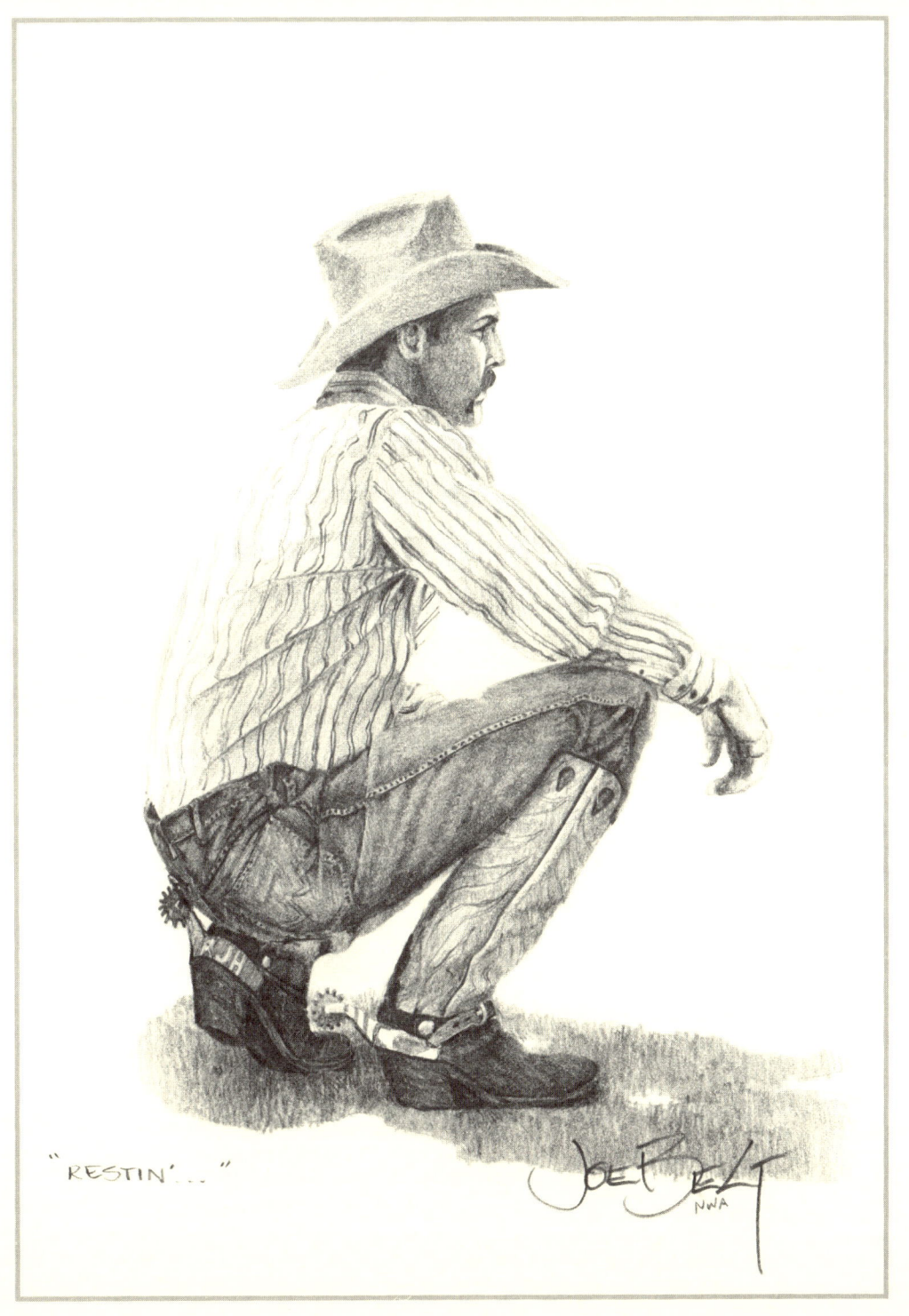

"RESTIN'..."

"LAZY SUMMER

15
LAZY SUMMER DAY, 1984
Before a ranch rodeo at Roaring Springs, Texas
12" x 20"
Craig Kelly
Lubbock, Texas

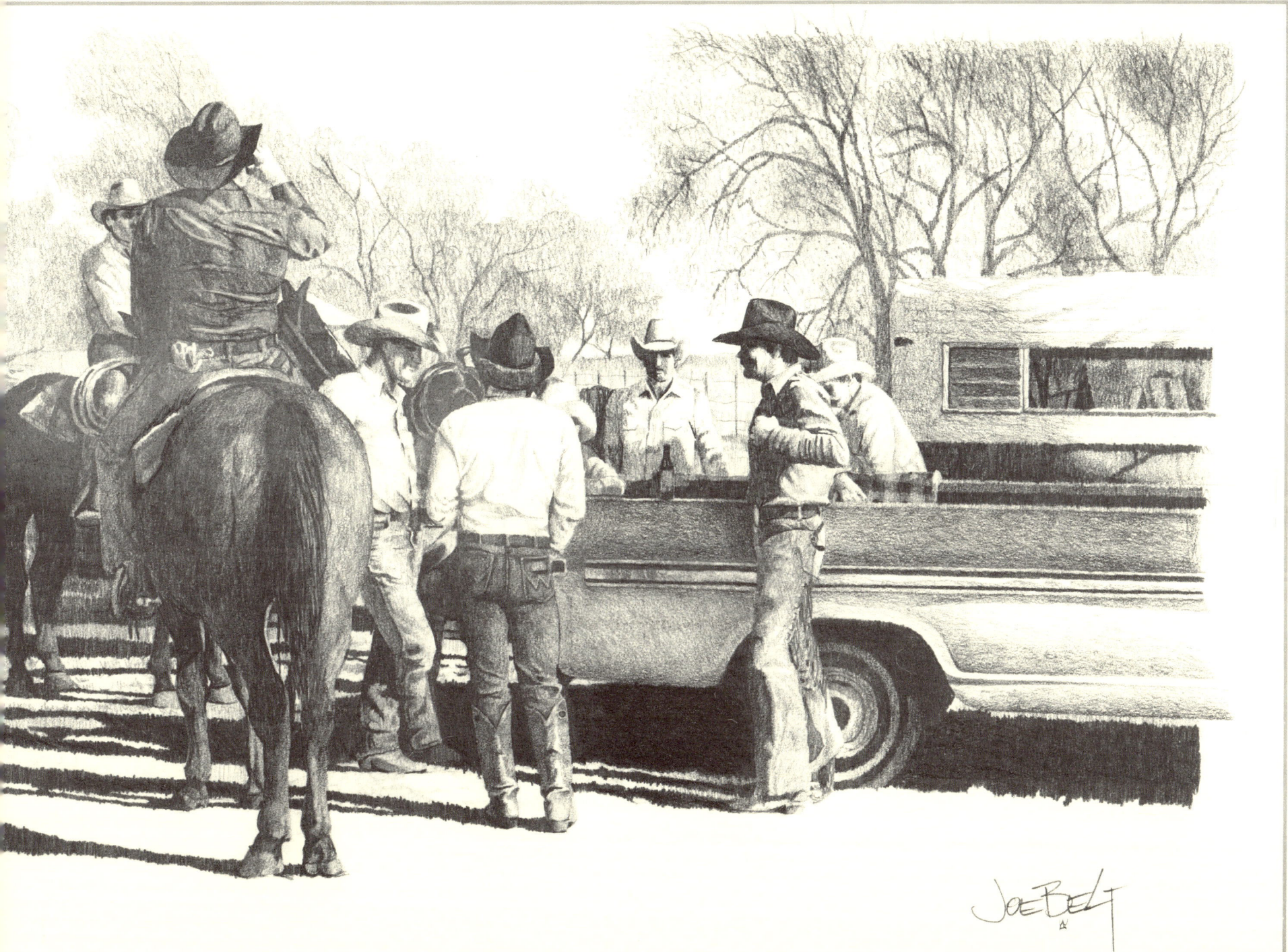

16

JUST RESTIN', 1987
Horse from the old Buffalo Springs Lake Riding Stables, Buffalo Springs, Texas
8" x 15"
Mr. and Mrs. Alvin Davis
Lubbock, Texas

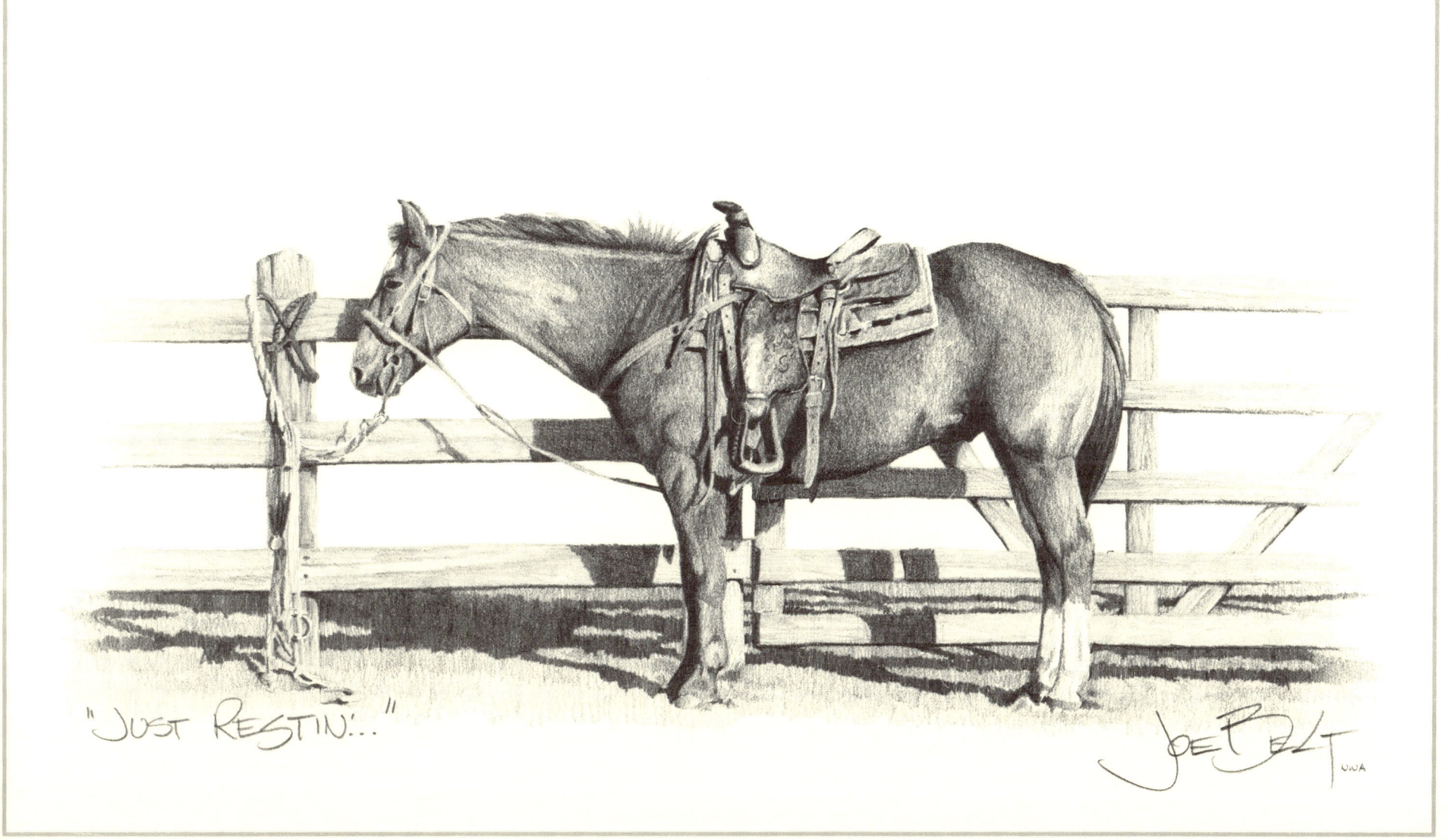

"JUST RESTIN'..."

Joe Belt
IOWA

17
Ol' Tut Garnett and His 86 Proof Pain Killer, 1983
Matador cowboy
7½" x 9½"
W. L. Sweatt
Colorado City, Texas

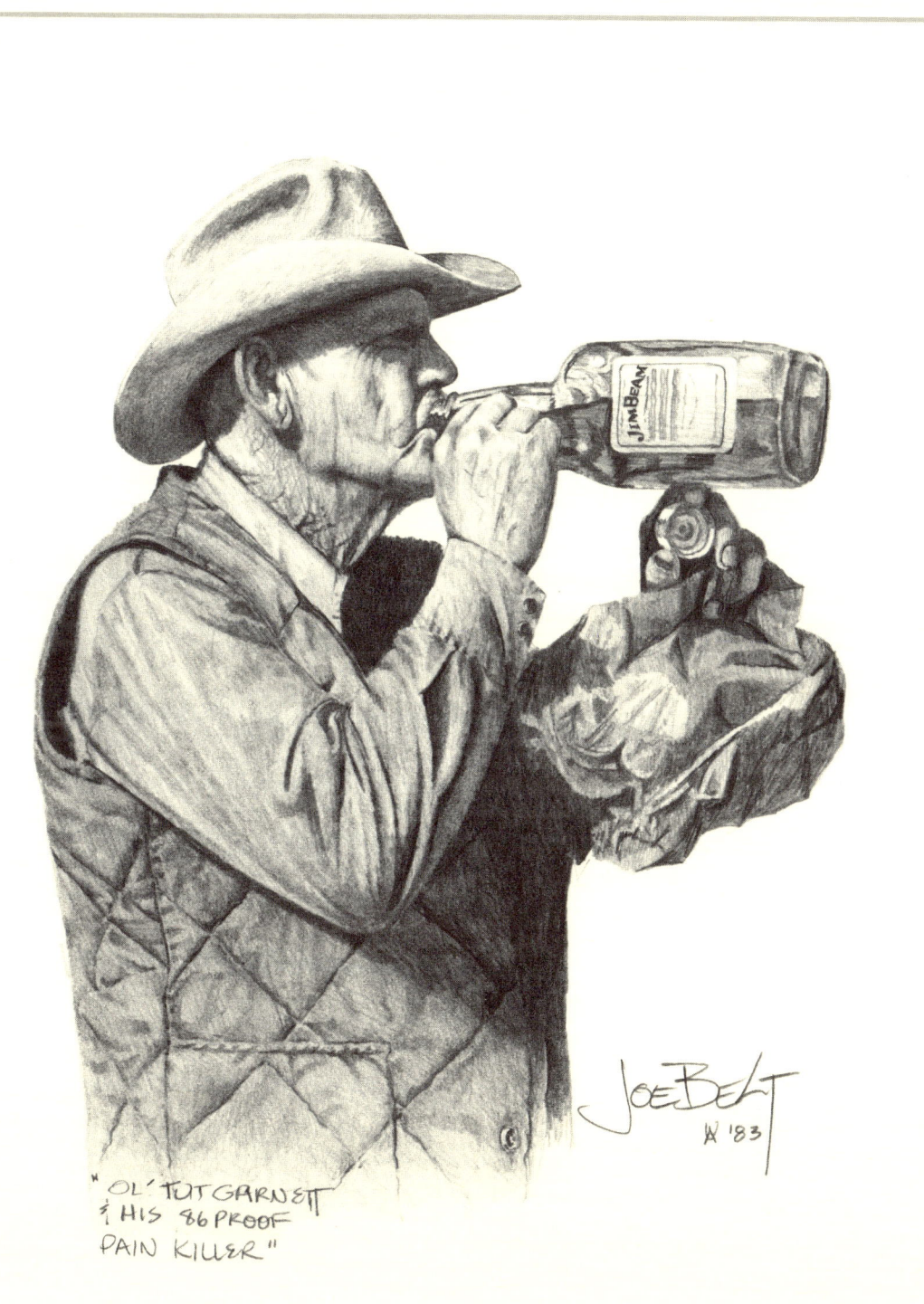

" OL' TUT GARNETT
& HIS 86 PROOF
PAIN KILLER "

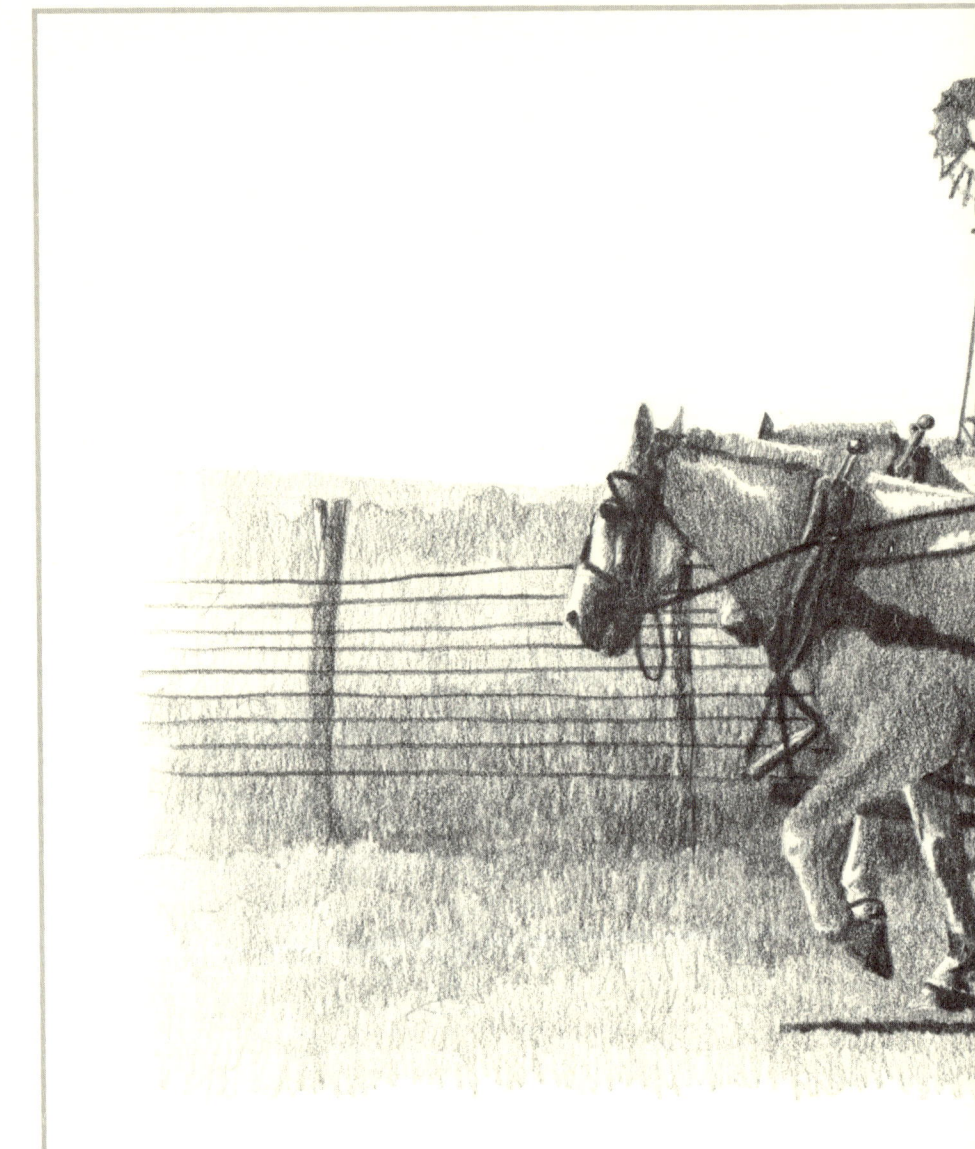

 MENDING FENCE, 1985
Riley and Willie working fences near Justiceburg, Texas
6" x 15¾"
First National Bank
Lubbock, Texas

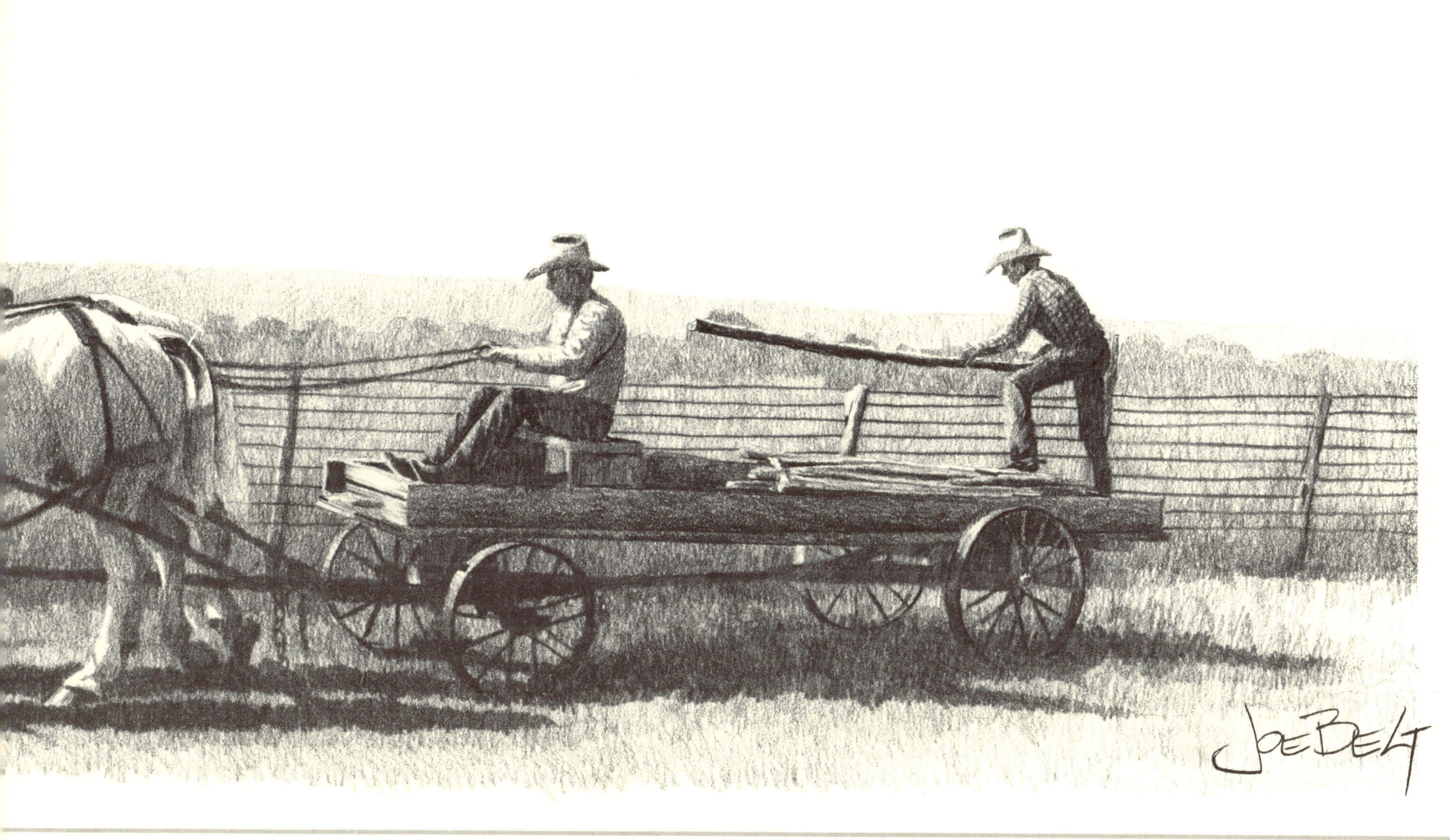

THE WINDMILL—THE SYMBOL OF THE PLAINS, 1981
Between Brownfield and Plains, Texas
17" x 23"
Joe Belt
Lubbock, Texas

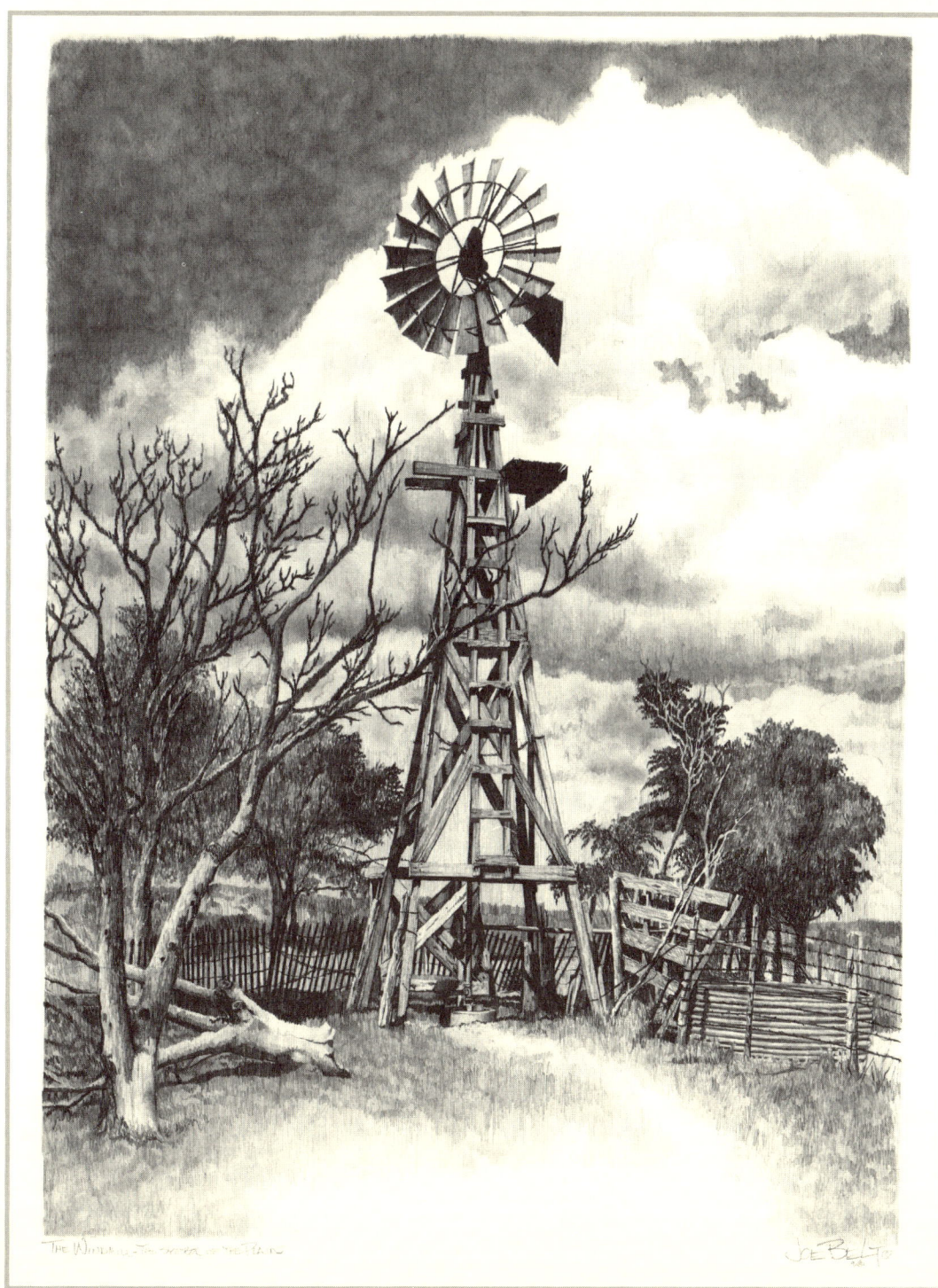

The Windmill, The Keeper of the Plains

20
KIOWA APACHE, 1987
16" x 21"
Joe Belt
Lubbock, Texas

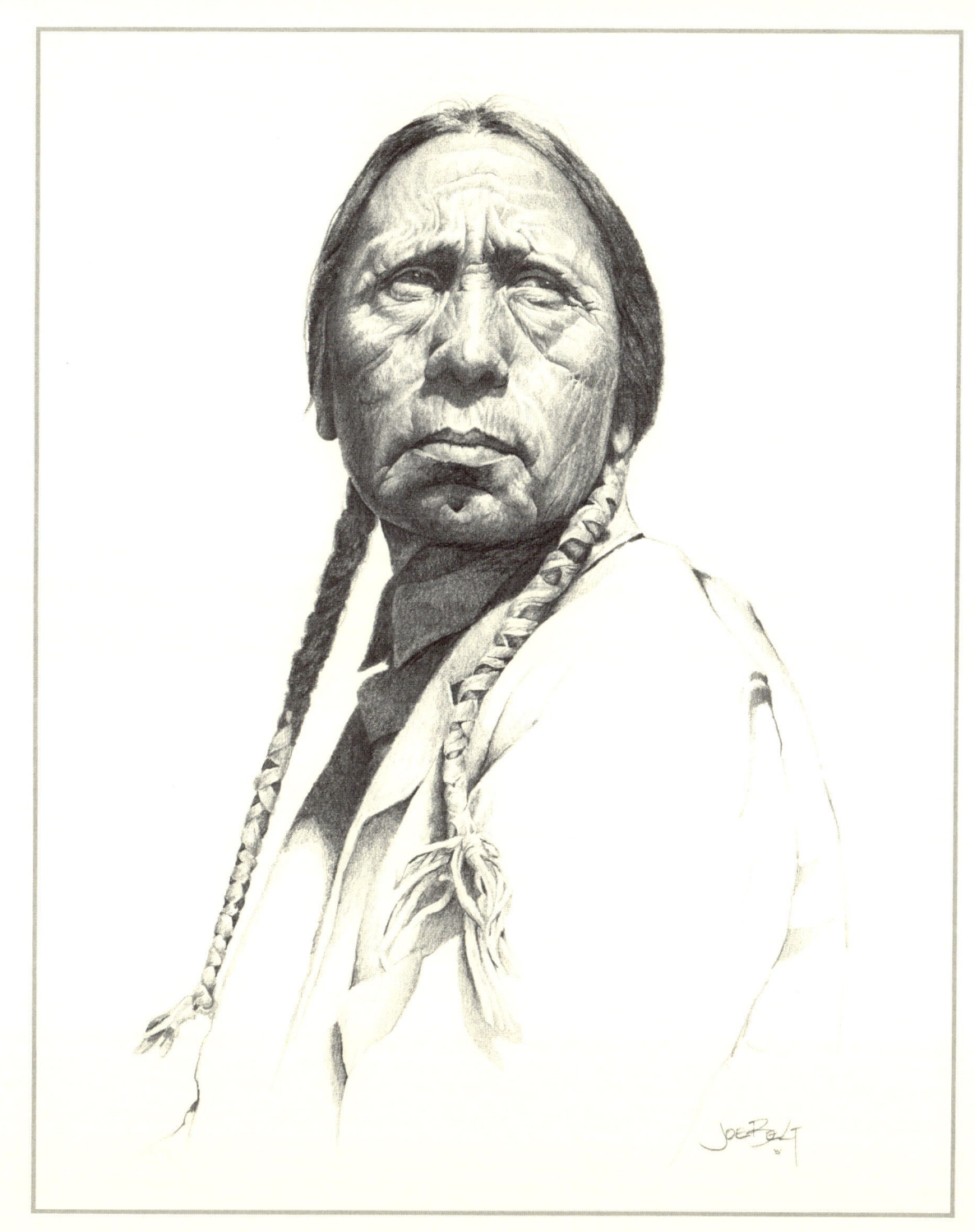

21

MATADOR ROUNDUP, 1984
Cowboys working cattle on the old Matador Ranch
16" x 22"
Mr. and Mrs. Norman Williamson
Lubbock, Texas

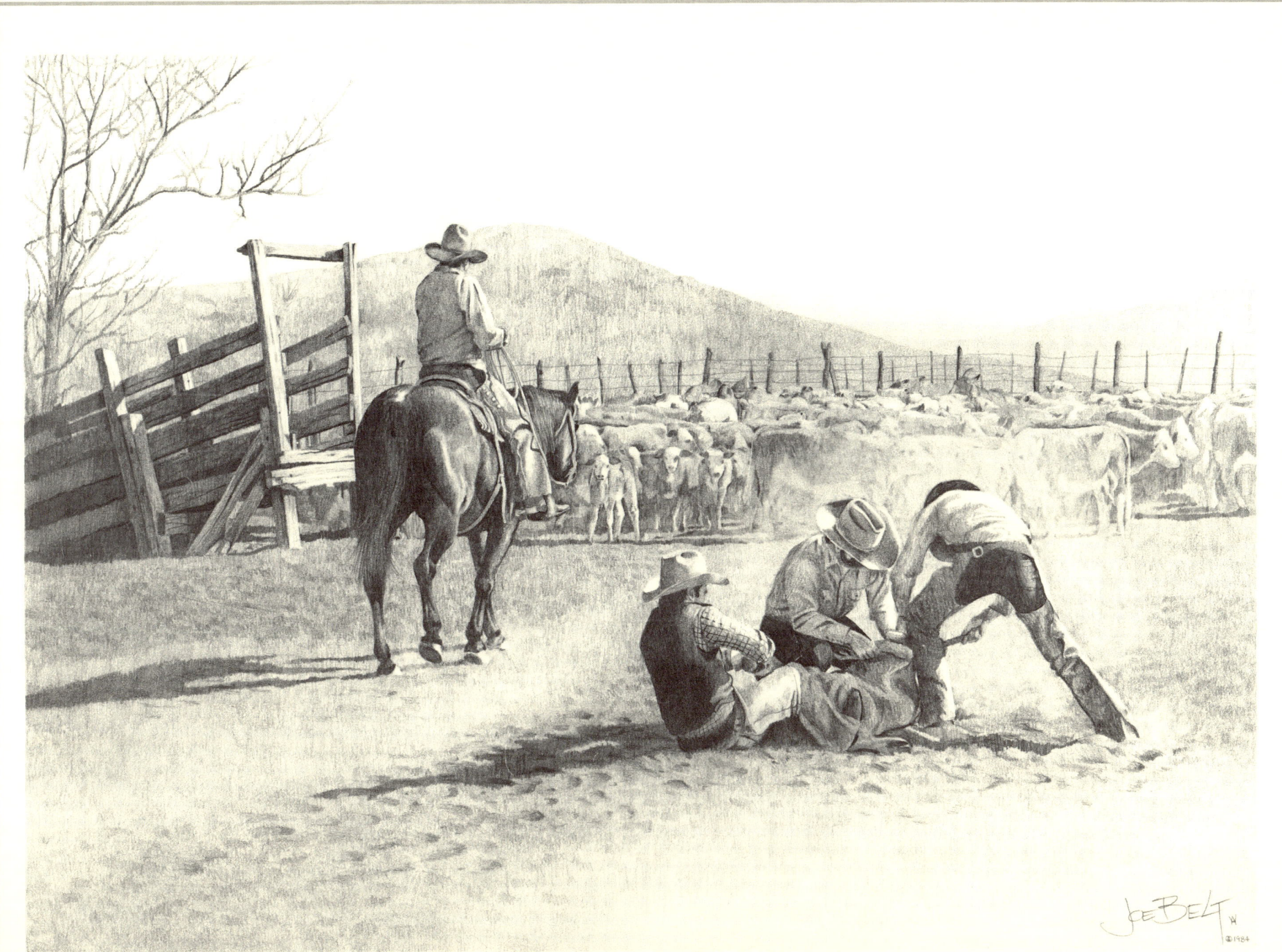

22

BRING 'EM ON, 1984
Cowboy working at the Matador Land and Cattle Co.
14" x 22"
Mr. and Mrs. David Tuohy
San Diego, California

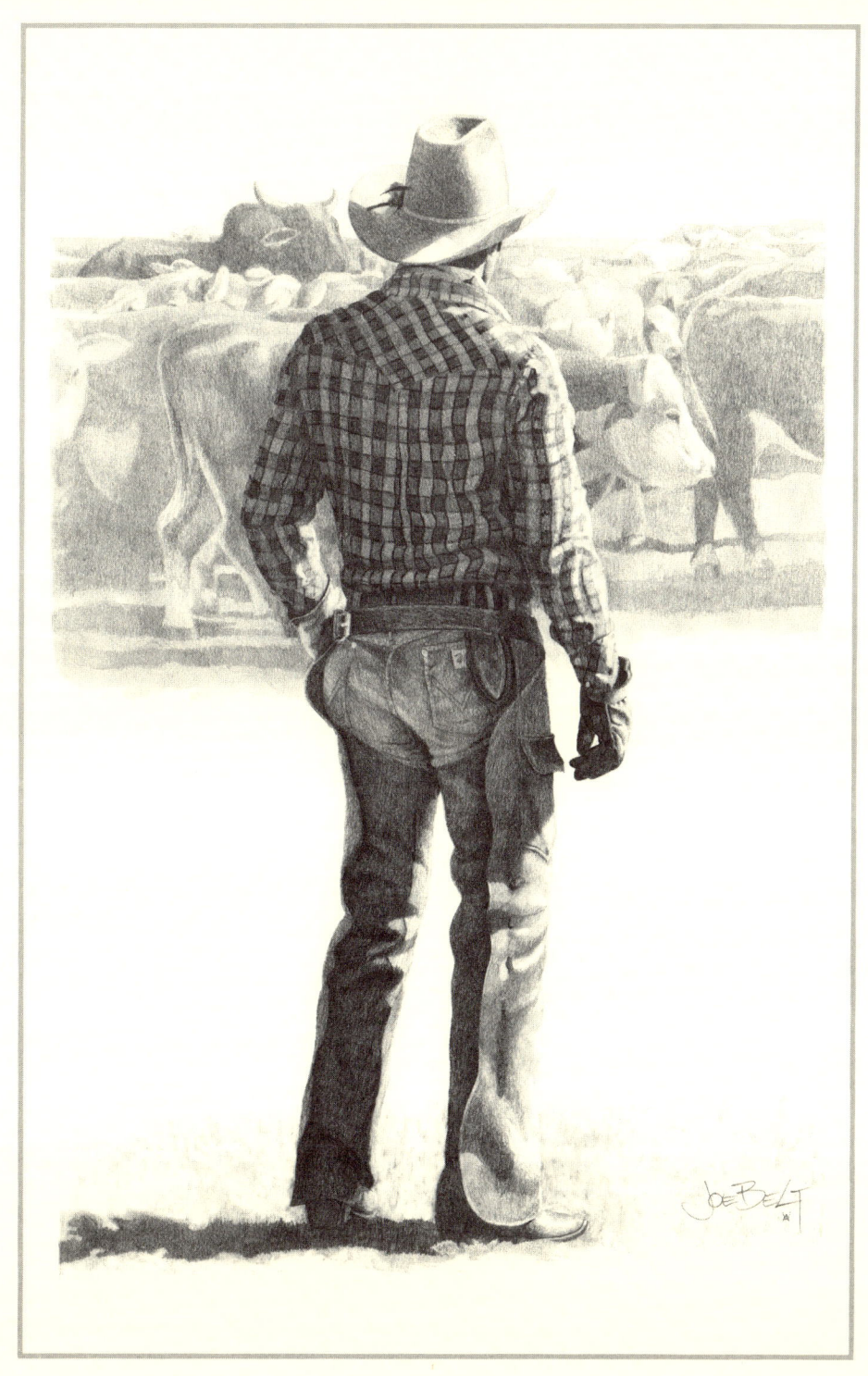

23
SHE-WITH-MANY-SMILES, 1985
Elderly Navajo Woman
11" x 20"
Mr. and Mrs. Mark Johnson
Lubbock, Texas

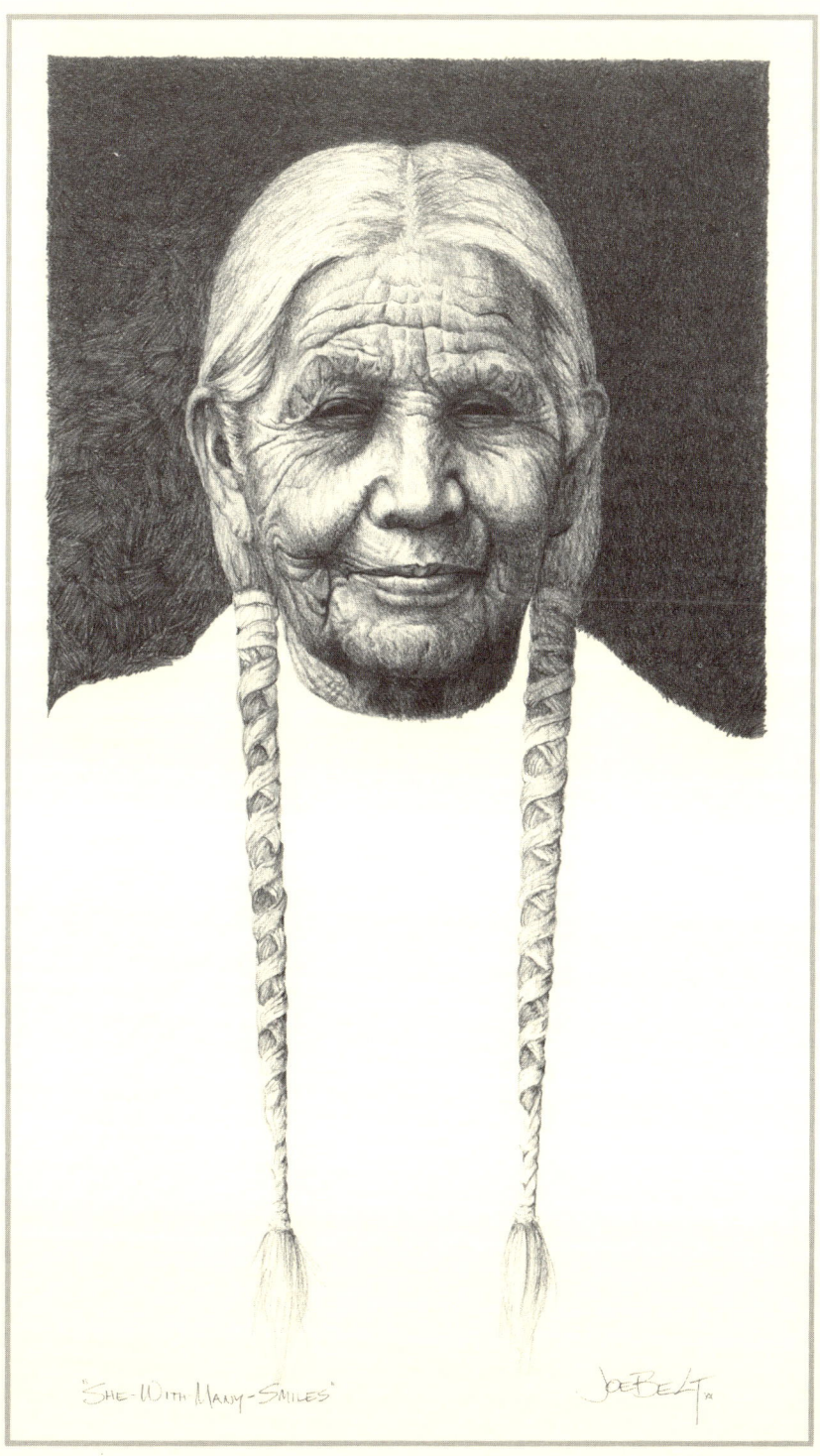

"She-With-Many-Smiles"   Joe Belt

OLE CHARLIE AND HIS BIG FORTY, 1984
One of the owners of Mesquite's Restaurant, Lubbock, Texas
14" x 24"
Mesquite's Restaurant
Lubbock, Texas

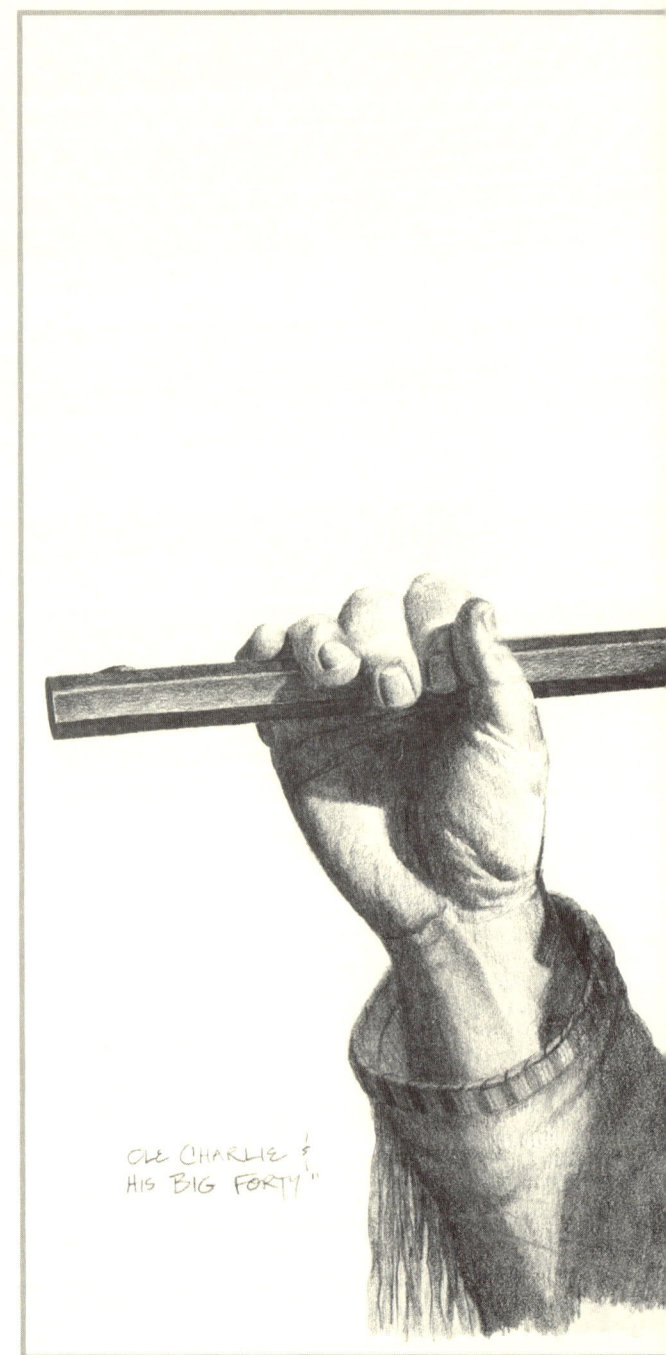

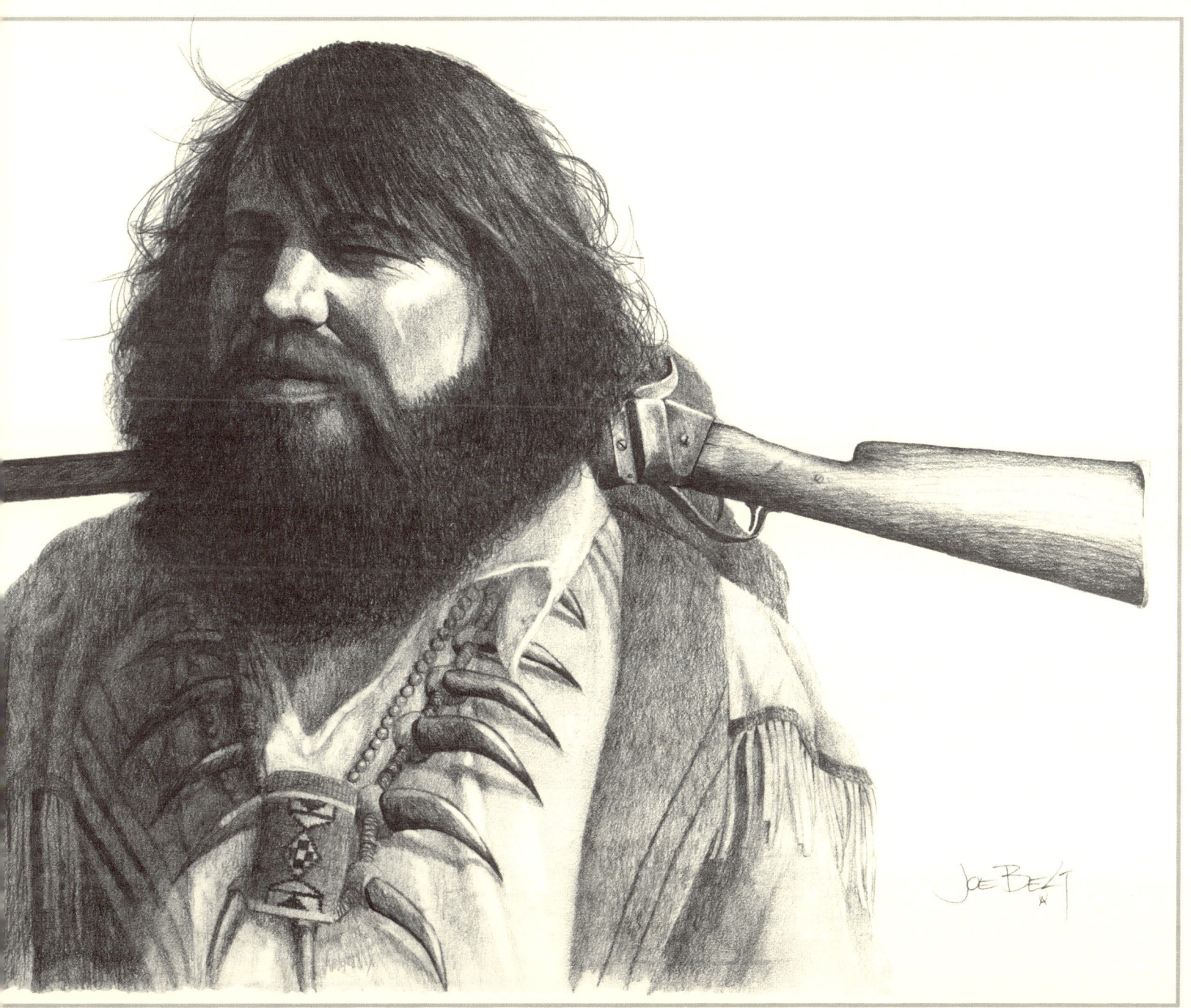

LARRY, 1987
An old friend from high school
20" x 28"
Mr. and Mrs. Mike Worley
Lubbock, Texas

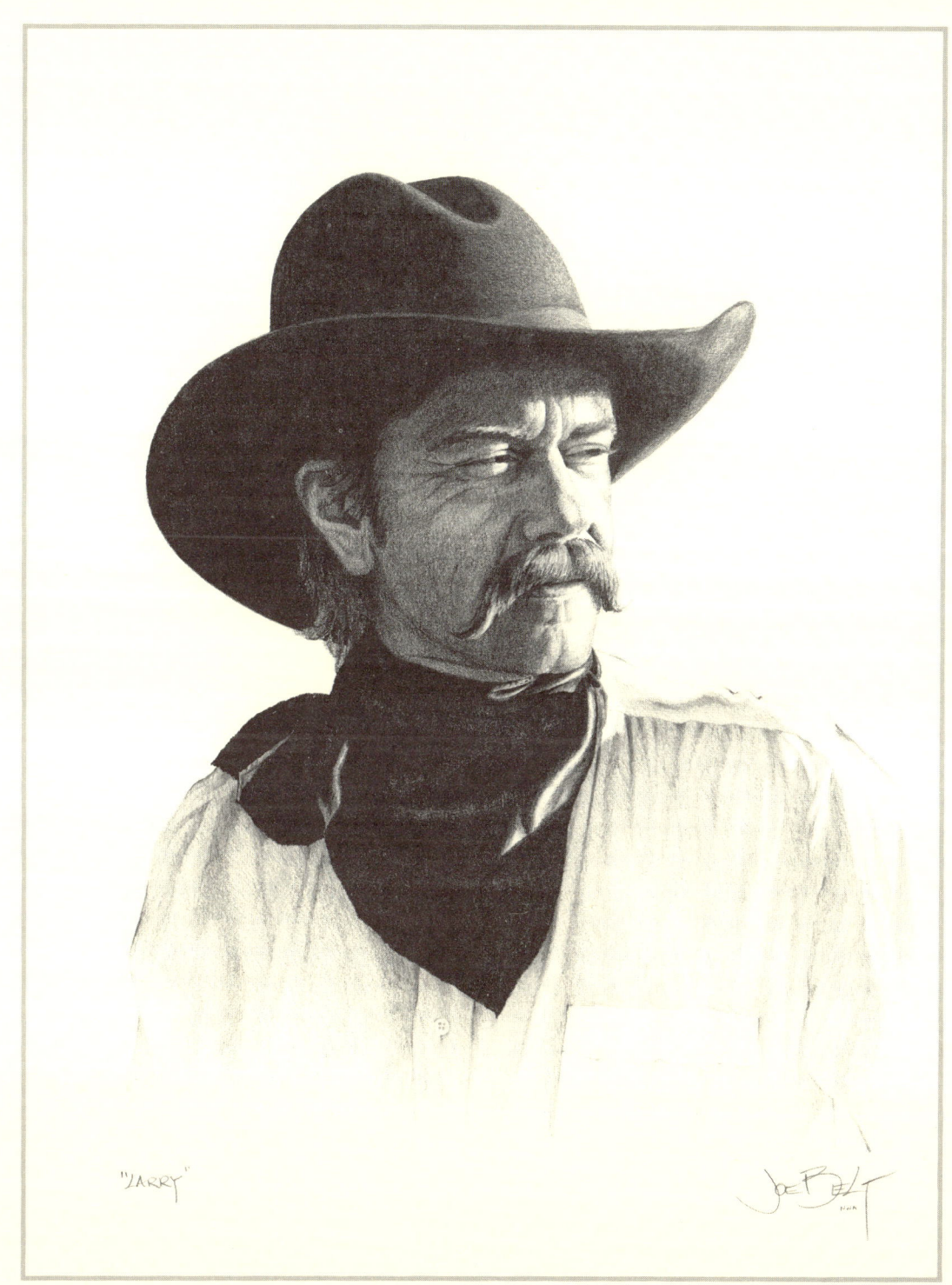

"LARRY"

Joe Belt
NWR

26

THE CONFRONTATION, 1983
A group of "mountain men" at a rendezvous near Justiceburg, Texas
12½" x 17"
Mr. and Mrs. David Tuohy
San Diego, California

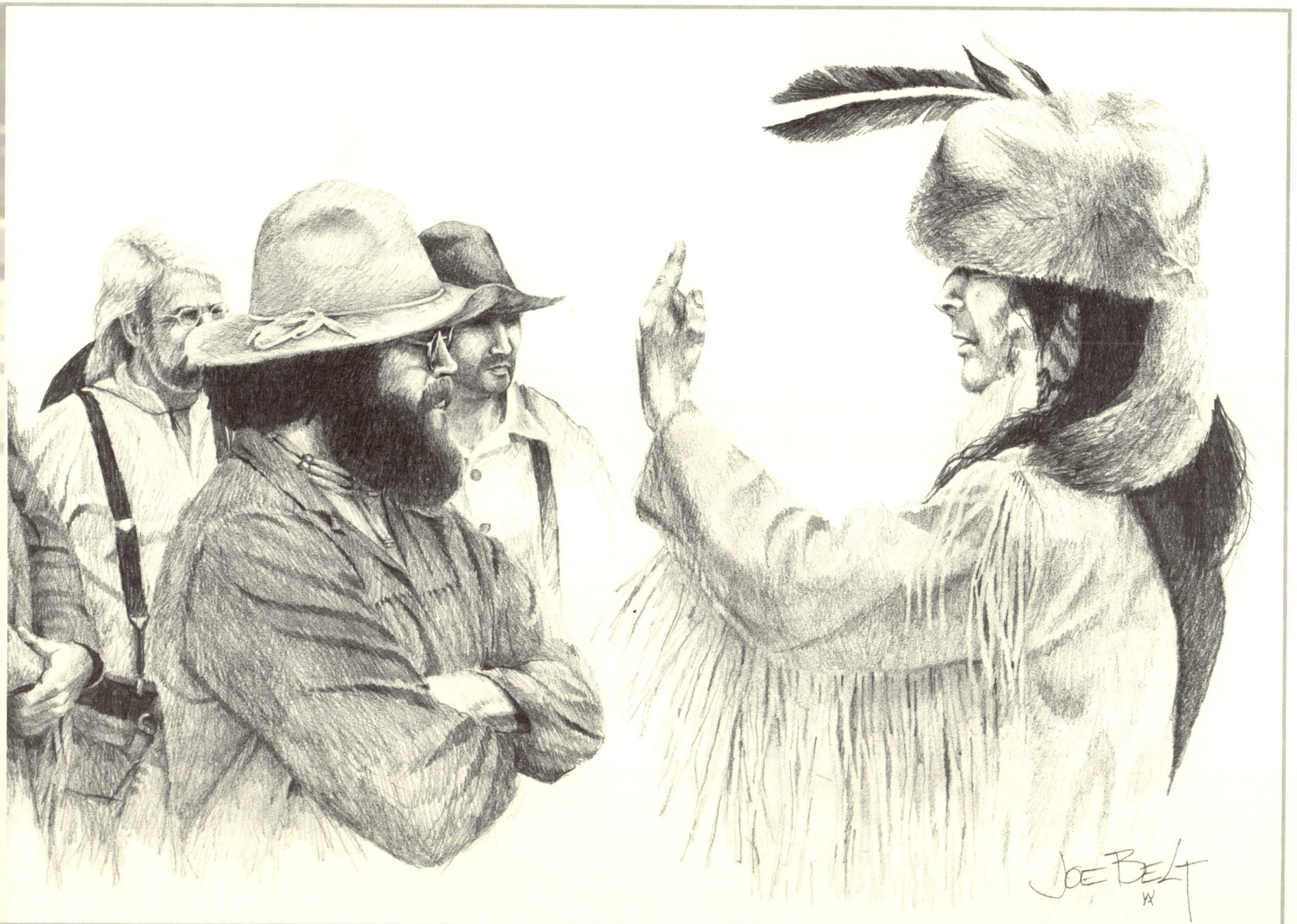

27
WHEREVER THE FOOT OF THE SHEEP TOUCHES, THE LAND TURNS TO GOLD, 1980
22" x 26"
Joe Belt
Lubbock, Texas

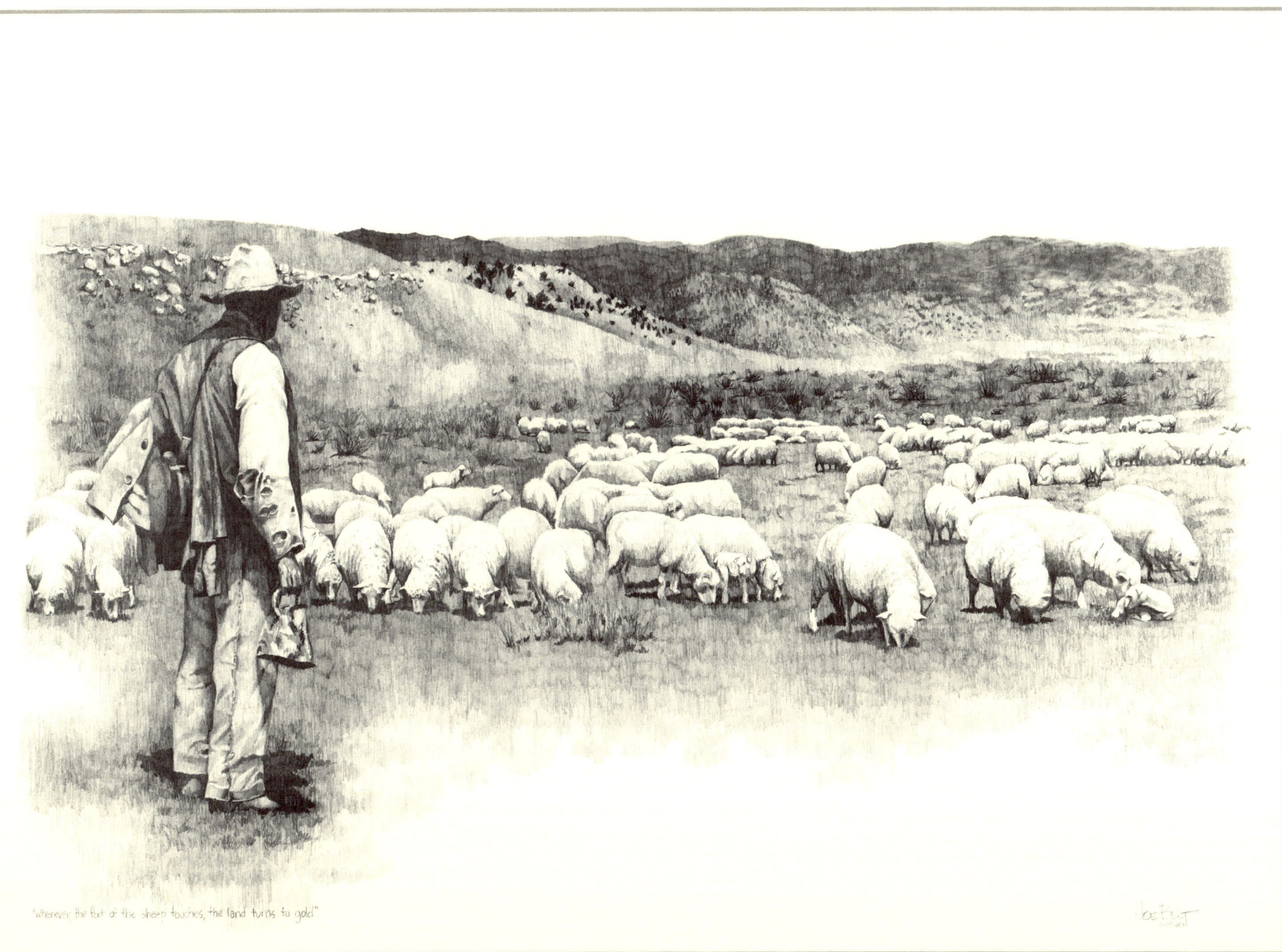

"Wherever the foot of the sheep touches, the land turns to gold"

K.D.—A PORTRAIT STUDY, 1987
An Oklahoma Indian
7" x 10½"
Mr. and Mrs. Jay Foreman
Lubbock, Texas

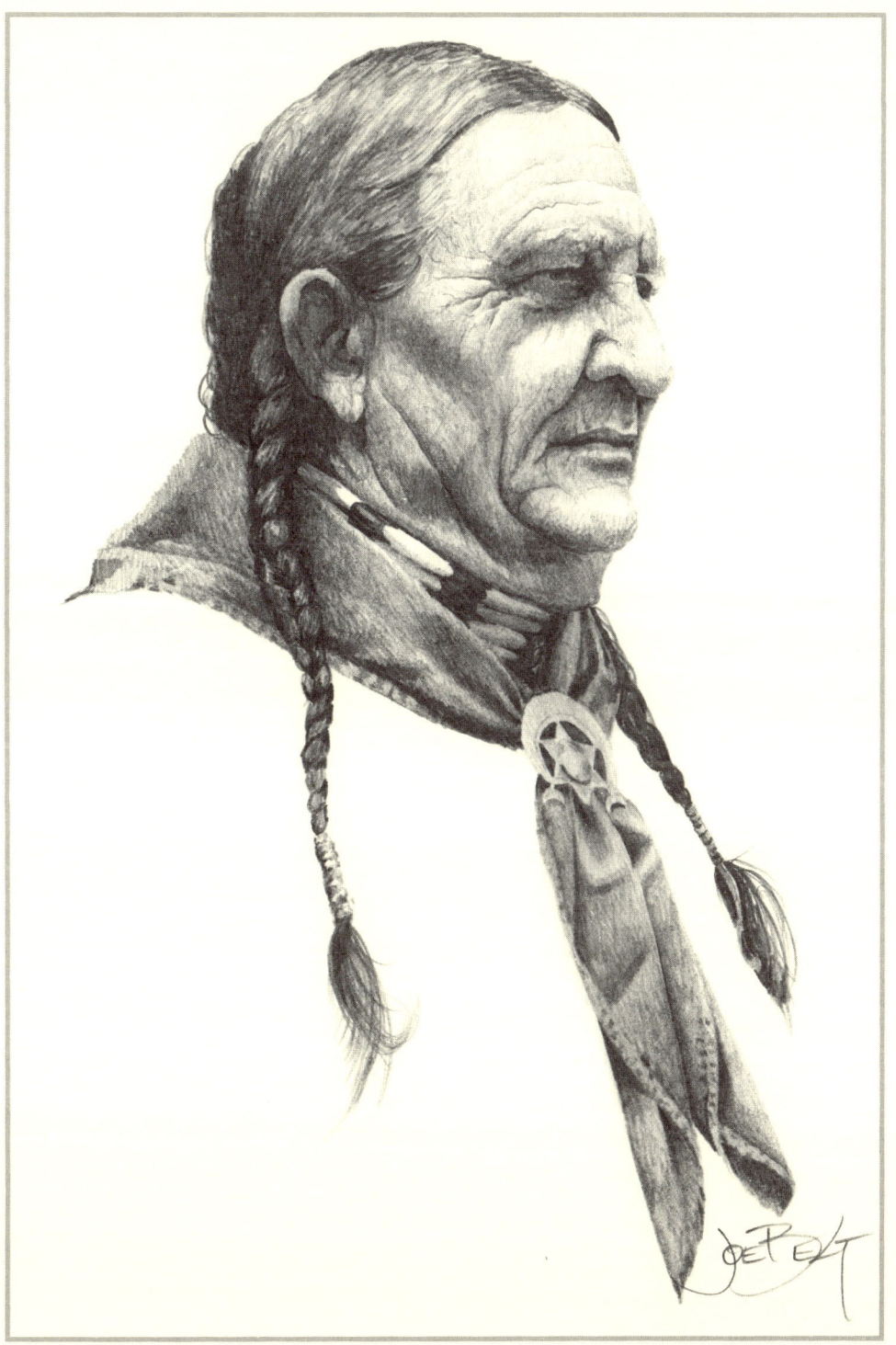

29
TRAILING A LEGEND, 1981
From the YO Ranch near Kerrville, Texas
20" x 28"
Gene Messer
Lubbock, Texas

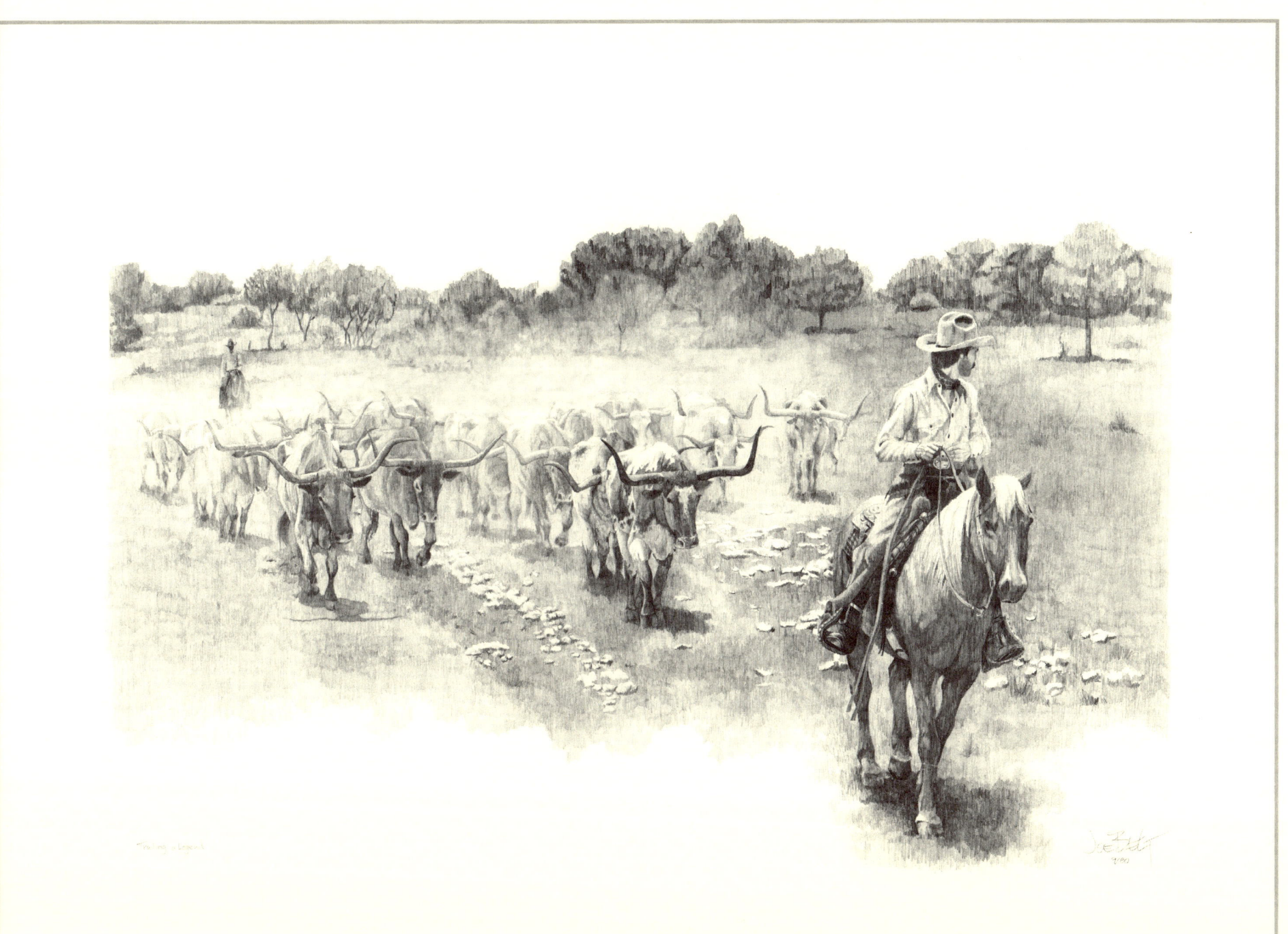

PORTRAIT STUDY—GRACIE, 1988
8" x 10"
Joe Belt
Lubbock, Texas

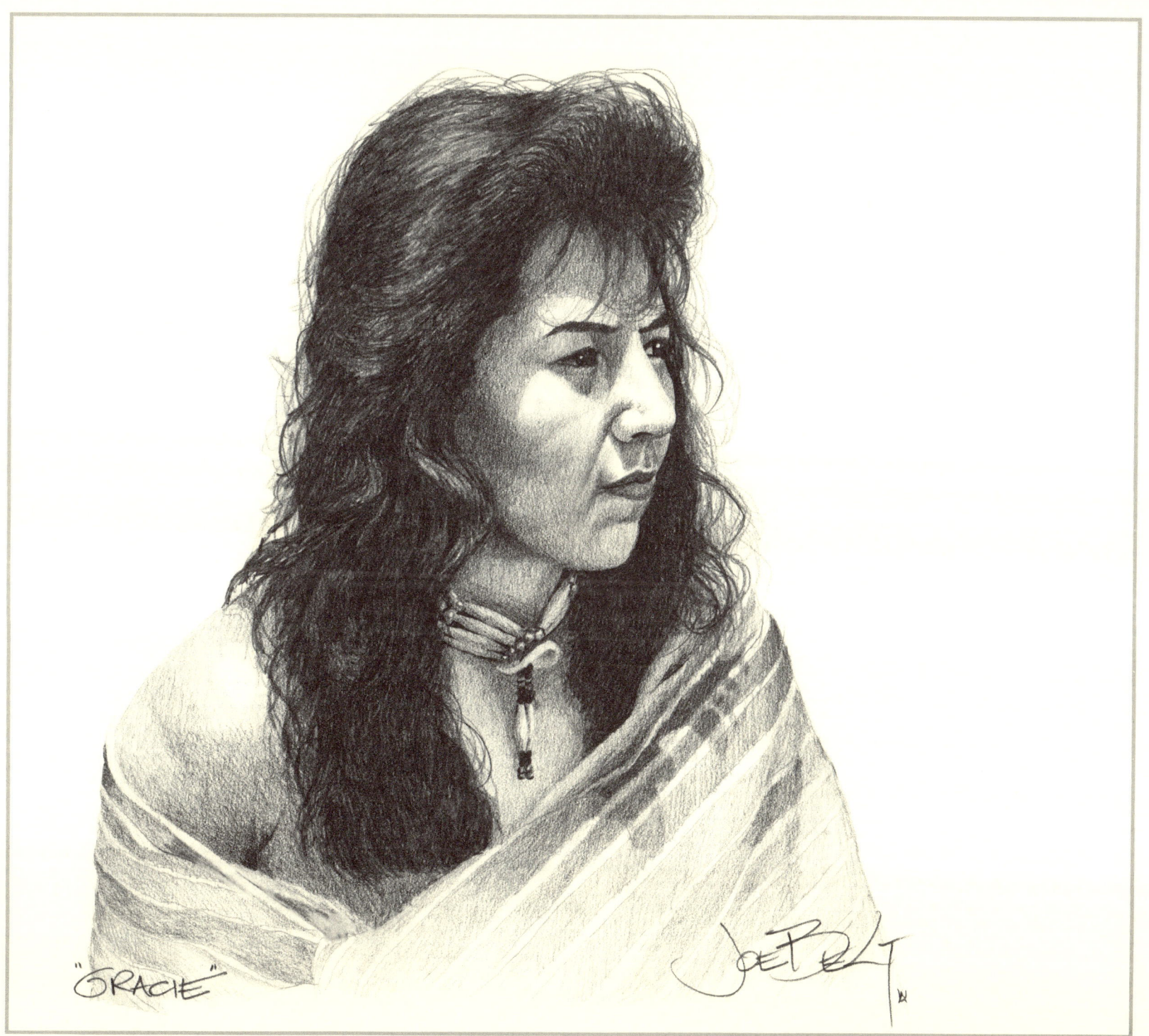

"GRACIE"

JoeBelt

31
DRUMMER—A STUDY, 1986
9" x 12"
Joe Belt
Lubbock, Texas

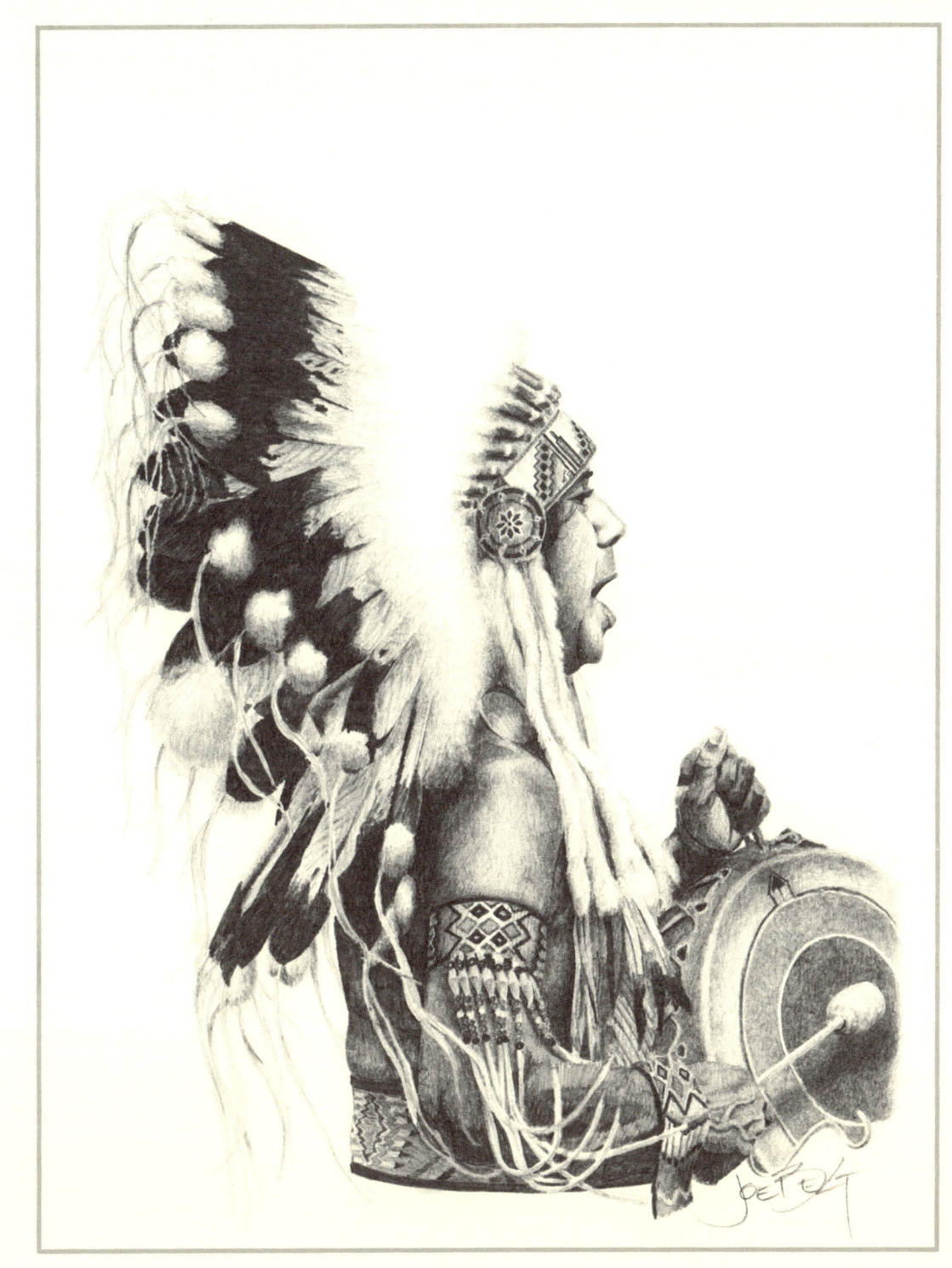

32
CALF ROPERS AT MESCALERO, NM 1984
11" x 14"
Mr. and Mrs. Mark Northcutt
Lubbock, Texas

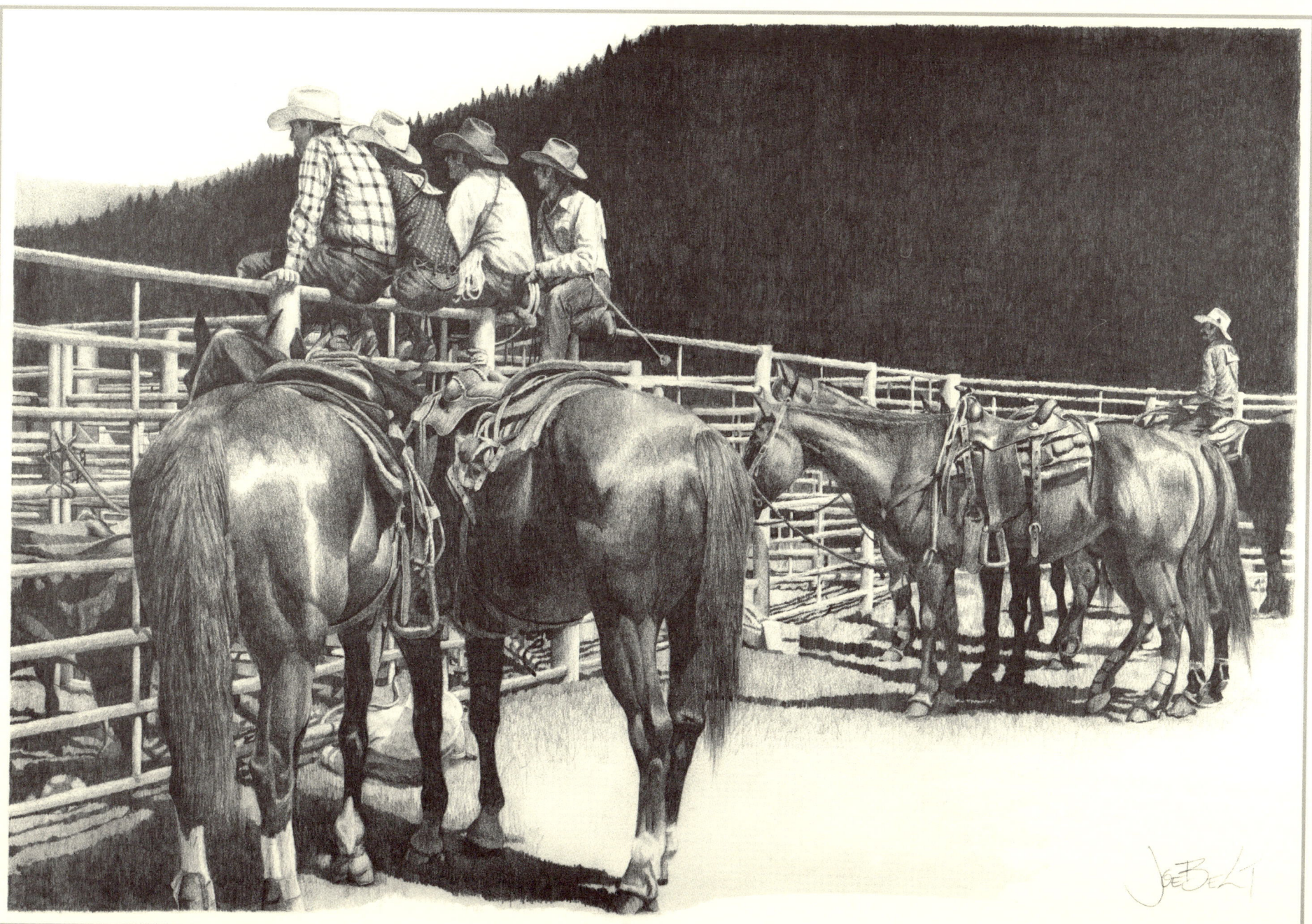

33
A YOUNG CROW INDIAN, 1983
11″ x 14″
Mr. and Mrs. George Maher
Lubbock, Texas

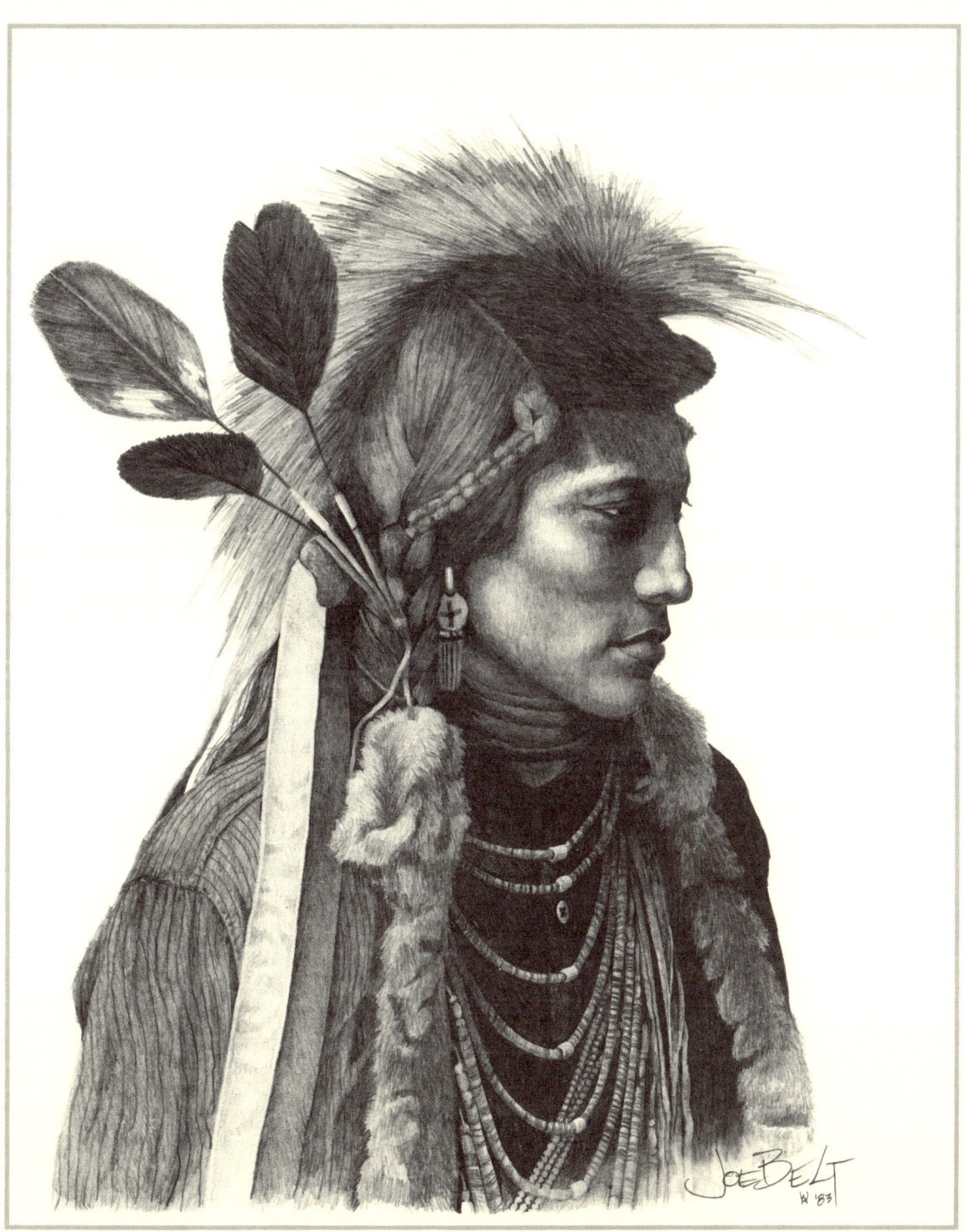

Designer: Pat Barrows Maines
Typeface: Lubalin Graph
Paper: Text—Strathmore Nantucket Ivory
        Cover—Curtis Flannel Khaki
Cloth: Buckram Centennial